# bread
# tomato
# garlic

# bread tomato garlic

jill dupleix

photography by geoff lung

SOMA

First published in Great Britain in 1999 by Conran Octopus Limited. North American edition published 1999 by Soma Books, by arrangement with Conran Octopus Limited.

Soma Books is an imprint of Bay Books & Tapes, 555 De Haro Street, No. 220, San Francisco, CA, 94107.

Text © 1999 Jill Dupleix
Photography © 1999 Conran Octopus
Design and layout © 1999 Conran Octopus
North American text © 1999 Soma Books

Library of Congress Cataloging-in-Publication data on file with the Publisher.

ISBN 1-57959-022-5

Printed in China

**For the Conran Octopus edition:**

**Commissioning Editor**  Suzannah Gough

**Consultant Food Editor**  Jenni Muir

**Editor**  Helen Woodhall

**Photographs**  Geoff Lung

**For the Soma edition:**

**Publisher**  James Connolly

**North American Editor**  Cynthia Nims

**Production**  Patrick Barber

**Proofreader**  Karen Stein

# contents

# introduction

Take three, and make yourself a meal ... prawns, chile, ginger; pork, apple, sage; sardines, arugula, red pepper; ricotta, honey, pine nuts.

Food is a language best kept simple, so let's keep it short, sweet and straight to the table. Let's put flavor and freshness before fuss and bother.

Let's make every ingredient count, by shopping well, by cooking fast and by eating slow. Let's think about color, texture and flavor, and let them contrast, collide and collaborate.

Each recipe in this book is built on three major players, with a small supporting cast to be found in any well-stocked pantry.

When you cook with very few ingredients, each one has to be a star, so get rid of that ugly crowd of extras hanging around and go for less food, more impact. Because the natural simplicity of food is the most civilized thing the world has to offer. Simple food is never boring. Simple food has balance and beauty. It is food at its best, in its natural shape and form. Taking something pure and raw and turning it into something exotic and unrecognizable is not what this is about. Besides, it takes too long.

Food that is bland and mass-produced is food that needs a lot more work and refinement to make it interesting. Why bother? Instead, start with the natural, fresh and unrefined produce.

Good food sets you free: like pasta, tomato, basil; chicken, ginger, soy; coffee, chocolate, rum. Take three, and remind yourself how simple life can be.

# food is a language best kept simple

The main thing to remember is that your three ingredients must be best friends: able to sleep together and still talk to each other in the morning. They don't have to be similar to be compatible, as anyone who has embarked on a long-term relationship (more than three days) will know.

Go for big flavors at the height of their ripeness.

Seek out punchy contrasts – steak with blue cheese; lemon with chicken; prosciutto with pears; lamb with pesto.

Combine flavors with a highly developed sense of menage à trois. Find that illicit third partner to make the original couple exciting. Chicken and arugula are yawn material until lemons come along.

Figs and honey are okay, but they soar when hit with tangy yogurt. Tuna and radicchio are desperate for crisp bacon.

Reduce and intensify flavors: oven-roast tomatoes, onions, beets, peppers and eggplant for an hour in a moderate oven until their water content reduces and flavors intensify.

Grill eggplant, zucchini, and red peppers. Marinate them in olive oil and herbs and use them in a hundred different ways.

Reduce the flavors of stocks, sauces, broths and juices by simmering, allowing the liquid to evaporate and intensify.

Roast the unroastable, and discover a new world of flavor: asparagus,

corn on the cob, carrots, zucchini, risotto, ricotta cheese, whatever. Particularly whatever.

Poach fruits, and use the cooking juices as a syrupy sauce. Reduce fruit juices into sticky syrups with a little sugar and spice.

Incorporate reduced flavors into butter or mayonnaise for instant flavor additives. Try Parmesan butter on pasta, avocado butter on prawns, saffron butter on fish.

Double up. If using lemon juice, grate the rind as well, and add a wedge to the plate. If there's bacon in there, crisp an extra slice and crumble on top. Don't throw out the leaves of baby beets: cook them and serve under the beets. It's called resource management and it's a smart thing to do.

# staples

You've got breakfast cereal, right? Then at least you won't starve. But we're talking about feeding yourself and others without getting embarassed. We're talking about having enough good things on hand to turn out a great meal in minutes.

We're not talking about starting your own specialty food shop; just about stocking up on the odd can of bamboo shoots and water chestnuts for instant stir-fries. Keeping a store of anchovies, capers, olives, sun-dried tomatoes and artichoke hearts for spontaneous weekend lunches. Feeding off a big wedge of Parmesan cheese in the fridge and having pasta, noodles and a few cans of tomatoes and tuna in the cupboard.

If you have onions and garlic, you can cook anything. Chiles are terrific. And, always, always, lemons, just in case you get a wild and crazy urge for a piece of grilled fish or a decent gin and tonic.

Feel free to use quality convenience foods like five-minute polenta, canned beans and somebody else's homemade pickles, with no added guilt. At least you're cooking.

You don't need all the stuff on this list. Build your pantry slowly, season by season. Stretch out the big investment items with more affordable everyday stuff. And always buy one thing you've never tried before in your life.

good cooking starts with good shopping

# fresh

**Buy these things regularly, or you will probably die.**

**Milk**  Fresh.

**Bread**  Great, long-lasting, naturally leavened sourdough.

**Butter**  Salted or unsalted, it's up to you.

**Eggs**  Free range, because it's nicer to the hens.

**Lemons**  Heavy and juicy. Warm them slightly before squeezing them to get extra juice.

**Onions**  White, yellow, red, whatever you like.

**Garlic**  Smash each clove with your fist, peel off the skin and cook. Fish it out later, if you remember.

# pantry

**Anchovy fillets** in oil.

**Apricots,** dried.

**Bamboo shoots,** canned. Drain and rinse. If they smell very bambooey, drop into boiling water for 2 minutes before using.

**Bamboo skewers**

**Bay leaves**

**Beans,** white, canned.

**Black beans,** salted. Fermented, salted black beans, available from Asian food stores. Rinse well before using.

**Black peppercorns**

**Bread crumbs,** dried.

**Capers,** small and salted.

**Chicken stock** in the freezer.

**Chiles,** dried – long, dried red chiles are a Malaysian staple. Hang them in your kitchen and they'll last forever. Either grind to a powder, or soak in hot water for an hour, then process in the food processor with a little of the water and add the purée to dishes.

**Chile oil** Available in small bottles of highly concentrated hot stuff from Asian food stores.

**Chinese rice wine** Known as *shao hsing*, this is the "cooking brandy" of China, used to add complexity and flavor by the spoonful. It costs very little and is available at Asian food stores. Or substitute dry sherry. I don't recommmend drinking it.

**Chinese shiitake mushrooms,** dried. Buy the neatest and largest type available, for the best flavor. Soak them in hot water for at least 30 minutes, then drain and cut off and discard the stem before using. You can use the soaking water to add flavor to dishes, but strain it first to get rid of any grit.

**Chocolate,** unsweetened cooking.

**Coffee beans**

**Cognac,** or your favorite liqueur.

**Cornstarch**

**Crisp-fried shallots** Small deep-fried shallots available by the jar in Asian food stores. Saves an awful lot of work.

**Five-spice powder** A premixed spice blend available from supermarkets and Asian food stores, usually made up of star anise, cinnamon, cloves, fennel and Sichuan peppercorns.

**Flour,** all-purpose.

**Herbs,** especially mint and oregano.

**Honey**

# ...music
## to cook by

**Instant dashi powder** Made of ground dried bonito (fish) and konbu (kelp), this is a wonderfully easy way of making the mother-stock of Japanese cooking. Available from Japanese food stores and health food stores. Mix 1 tablespoon of instant dashi powder with 2 cups hot water.

**Mayonnaise,** premium brand.

**Mirin** Sweet Japanese rice wine, available from Asian food stores.

**Music,** to cook by.

**Mustard,** Dijon.

**Oils** Extra-virgin olive oil, vegetable or peanut oil, sesame oil.

**Oyster sauce** Dark, thick, oyster-flavored sauce thickened with cornstarch, available from Asian food stores.

vodka in the freezer for drinking

**Parmesan cheese,** preferably in a wedge.

**Pasta,** dried. Your favorites.

**Pernod,** an anise liqueur.

**Pickled onions**

**Rice,** Arborio, jasmine, basmati.

**Rice wine vinegar** A mild, sweet vinegar made from fermented rice. Substitute with a good white wine vinegar.

**Saffron threads**

**Sake** A clear wine brewed from rice used in Japanese cooking. Cooking sake is available from Asian food stores.

**Salmon** canned in oil, premium brand.

**Sansho chile pepper,** Japanese. The ground, dried red pod of the prickly ash, used to add heat to many Japanese dishes.

**Sea salt**

**Sesame oil** A rich, powerful oil made of hulled, toasted sesame seeds. Use

sparingly in Chinese cooking.

**Soy sauce** A fermented soybean product, available in both light (thin and salty) or dark (aged, less salty). If in doubt, use Japanese soy.

**Spices,** caraway seeds, ground cumin, ground coriander, cinnamon sticks, whole nutmeg, paprika.

**Sugar,** brown, granulated, confectioner's.

**Sweet chile sauce** A thick, sweet, seedy chile sauce used in Thai cooking.

**Tea leaves,** green.

**Thai fish sauce** A thin, dark, pungent, and quite salty sauce made from fermented fish (*nuoc mam* in Vietnam, *nam pla* in Thailand, *patis* in the Philippines).

**Tomato paste**

**Tomato ketchup**

**Tomatoes,** canned.

**Tuna**, canned in oil, premium brand.

**Vanilla beans**

**Vinegar,** balsamic, red wine, white wine.

**Vodka,** in the freezer, for drinking.

**Water chestnuts** The crisp round corms of a type of watergrass, available fresh or canned.

**Wine,** red and white, for drinking and cooking.

**Salt** is sea salt.

**Pepper** is freshly ground black pepper.

**Olive oil** is extra-virgin for salads and drizzling, and light for frying, changing to peanut or vegetable oil for Asian dishes.

**Sugar** is normal old white table sugar or brown sugar.

An **egg** is large.

A knob of **fresh ginger** is around 1 inch.

**Tomatoes** and **corn** are canned or fresh.

To **simmer** is to cook at a gentle bubble, not a rolling boil.

**The day you** leave your cereal box behind is the day you really grow up. And the day you leap out of bed and whisk gracefully into the kitchen to create a minor masterpiece without the slightest mess is the day you will never live to see. The thing is, it's morning. Sadly, breakfast comes at a time when you are at your most vulnerable. (Read: mascara smudges, bad hair, can't find kitchen.) You've just woken up. You're not up to speed yet. So go easy on yourself. Stack avocado and bacon on thick toast. Dollop yogurt on fruit crumble. Feast on a ripe mango. Still not awake? Then have your breakfast for lunch instead. But don't let anyone else cook you breakfast without thorough research into their habits, religion, background and sexual preferences. Breakfast is personal. Besides, they don't know where the coffee is, or how you like your toast. (Nor do you sometimes, but that's another matter.) Likewise, don't ever cook breakfast in bed for anyone else. It's far too presumptuous.

# breakfast

corn

basil

tomato

# crunchy corn fritters, sautéed tomatoes and fresh basil make a meal to look forward to all night

**main players:**

*2 ears corn, or 1 pound canned corn kernels,*
*drained*

*1 large bunch basil*

*1 pound ripe tomatoes*

**supporting cast:**

*2 tablespoons extra-virgin olive oil*

*2/3 cup milk*

*1 cup all-purpose flour, sifted*

*2 eggs*

*1/2 teaspoon paprika*

*1 teaspoon baking powder*

*1 teaspoon sugar*

*sea salt and freshly ground black pepper*

Peel the husks from the corn and use a sharp knife to shear the kernels from each ear. Wash the basil and shake dry. Pick off about 20 leaves and slice them into fine shreds. Slice the tomatoes thickly.

Heat half the oil in a nonstick frying pan and sauté the tomatoes over medium heat on both sides until lightly golden and soft. Set aside in a warm place.

Combine the shredded basil, milk, flour, eggs, paprika, baking powder, sugar, salt and pepper in a large bowl and stir well to make a smooth, thick batter.

Put corn kernels in a bowl and add enough batter to just cover them – keep it ridiculously corn kernelly – and toss to coat.

Heat the remaining oil in a nonstick frying pan until hot and drop 4 large spoonfuls of the mixture into the pan. Fry until golden, turning once. Keep the corn fritters warm while making four more.

Stack the corn fritters with tomato on each warmed serving plate and serve with extra sprigs of basil. **Serves four**

# a golden omelet folded over smoky grilled asparagus and melting goat cheese

eggs

asparagus

cheese

**main players:**

*1 pound thin asparagus, trimmed*

*5 ounces fresh goat cheese*

*12 eggs*

**supporting cast:**

*2 tablespoons extra-virgin olive oil*

*2 tablespoons butter*

*sea salt and freshly ground black pepper*

Brush the asparagus with olive oil and scatter with salt and pepper. Broil it, or cook it on a ridged cast-iron griddle, for 5–10 minutes, turning once, until tender.

Slice the cheese into eight slices. Set aside.

For each omelet, break 3 eggs into a bowl, season with salt and pepper and beat lightly with a fork. Heat a quarter of the butter in a nonstick frying pan until it foams. Pour in the eggs and cook over a medium heat. As the edges set, draw them back with a fork and allow the egg to run underneath and cook.

When the omelet is very nearly set, place two slices of cheese on one half of the surface and top with a layer of warm asparagus. Tip the pan slightly and fold over the top of the omelet with a fork, then slide it onto a warm plate and serve. Wipe out the pan, add a little more butter, and repeat for the remaining omelets.

**Makes four omelets**

avocado

bacon

toast

# a fast stack of creamy avocado, crisp bacon and warm tomatoes on garlicky toasted bread

**main players:**

*8 thin slices bacon*

*4 thick slices sourdough bread*

*1 avocado*

**supporting cast:**

*14-ounce can whole plum (roma) tomatoes*

*1 garlic clove, peeled and cut in half*

*1 tablespoon olive oil*

*sea salt and freshly ground black pepper*

Arrange the bacon on a foil-covered baking sheet and broil until crisp – or fry in a non-stick frying pan. Drain on paper towels.

Gently remove the whole tomatoes from the can, without breaking them, and heat over a low heat in a saucepan until warm.

Toast the bread on both sides, then rub one side with the cut clove of garlic and brush it with a little olive oil.

Meanwhile, cut the avocado in half and remove the pit. Peel off the skin and cut each half into thick slices.

Place the toasted bread on serving plates and top with the bacon and avocado. Sprinkle with salt and pepper, and top with tomatoes and more bacon. Serve hot.

**Serves four**

peaches

# summer fruit topped with a crunchy muesli crumble, served up warm in the morning

figs

muesli

**main players:**

6 ripe peaches

6 ripe figs

1 cup muesli

**supporting cast:**

1 tablespoon sugar for fruit, plus

   2 tablespoons for crumble

6 tablespoons butter

¾ cup all-purpose flour

Heat oven to 400°F. Wash and dry the peaches and figs. Cut the peaches into bite-size chunks, discarding pits, but do not peel. Cut the figs lengthwise into quarters. Arrange in a rough tumble in a shallow buttered pie dish or baking sheet. Sprinkle sugar over the top.

Cut the butter into tiny pieces and combine with the flour in a bowl. Rub the flour and butter together with your fingertips until clumpy. Mix with the muesli and sugar. Sprinkle with a little water and mix it through with a fork, leaving it quite lumpy.

Sprinkle the crumble topping on top of the fruit, and bake for about 40 minutes, until the fruit is bubbling hot and the topping is lightly golden.

Serve hot, warm or cold. **Serves four**

top rich, buttery toast with **smoked salmon** and a scramble of egg for a lazy Sunday breakfast of **simple luxury**

eggs

salmon

brioche

**main players:**

*1 loaf brioche or sourdough bread*

*10 eggs*

*8 slices smoked salmon*

**supporting cast:**

*2 tablespoons milk*

*2 tablespoons butter, plus extra for spreading*

*sea salt and freshly ground black pepper*

Cut four thick slices of bread and set aside.

Break the eggs into a bowl and add the milk, salt and pepper. Gently break up the eggs with a fork.

Melt the butter in a nonstick frying pan, and scramble the eggs over a fairly low heat, stirring and scraping constantly with a wooden spoon, until they are cooked but still moist and bouncy. Meanwhile, toast the bread, being careful not to burn it.

Butter the toast and arrange on serving plates. Top with soft folds of smoked salmon, and great spoonfuls of scrambled egg. Serve immediately. **Serves four**

# panettone

# plums

# yogurt

grilled Italian **fruit bread** served with a sweet compote of plums and **plenty** of yogurt

**main players:**

*1 pound red plums*

*1 panettone, or other fruit bread*

*1¼ cups plain yogurt*

**supporting cast:**

*1 cup sugar*

*1 cinnamon stick*

*1 vanilla bean, split*

Combine the sugar, cinnamon stick and vanilla bean with 2 cups of cold water in a small pan and heat, stirring, until the sugar has fully dissolved. Add the plums and poach gently for 10–15 minutes until tender. Their skins will slide off happily as they cook. Allow the plums to cool in the syrup, then remove them, and strain the syrup to remove the skins. Return the plums to the strained syrup. If you are superorganized, do this the night before.

Cut the panettone horizontally into 4 round slices about 1 inch thick, and set aside.

Heat the broiler, and toast the panettone on both sides, watching carefully, because it burns very easily. See? It burned in the time it took to read that last sentence.

Arrange freshly toasted, unburnt panettone on serving plates and top with poached plums and their syrup. Top with yogurt and serve. **Serves four**

the Sunday roast: a perfectly **poached egg** on top of sizzled bacon and **soft, sweet** roasted squash

**main players:**

*1 pound winter squash*

*8 thin slices prosciutto, bacon or pancetta*

*4 eggs*

**supporting cast:**

*2 tablespoon extra-virgin olive oil*

*2 tablespoon white wine vinegar*

*sea salt and freshly ground black pepper*

Heat oven to 400°F. Hack the squash into four chunky wedges (peel it if you like, but you don't have to), seed it and arrange on a baking sheet. Sprinkle with salt and pepper and drizzle with olive oil. Bake for an hour until the wedges are soft and golden brown.

Arrange the prosciutto or bacon slices on a sheet of foil, then bake or broil for a few minutes until crisp.

To poach the eggs, fill a wide shallow pan with water to a depth of 2 inches and bring to a rolling boil. Add the vinegar, which will help the whites to set. Turn off the heat, crack open an egg and drop it quickly but carefully into the water. Repeat with the remaining eggs.

Cover the pan immediately and check after 3 minutes. The whites should be set, but the yolk should still be soft and runny.

squash

Remove with a slotted spoon and drain on several folds of paper towels. Trim any messy edges with scissors.

Arrange the squash on four serving plates, tuck in the prosciutto or bacon slices, and top with a poached egg.

**Serves four**

prosciutto

egg

rice

prunes

figs

a bowl of **creamy risotto** studded with fat, juicy prunes and figs leaves boxed cereal for dead

**main players:**

1¼ cups Arborio rice

7 ounces pitted prunes

7 ounces dried figs

**supporting cast:**

4 cups milk

1 vanilla bean, split

1 cup brown sugar

Heat the milk and vanilla bean to a simmer. Add the rice and cook for 2–3 minutes, stirring, then reduce heat to very low – and I mean very low, or the whole thing will boil up and over – and cover. Cook gently for 15 minutes until the rice is tender and almost all of the milk has been absorbed, stirring occasionally.

In the meantime, combine 1 cup water with the sugar in a small pan and bring to a boil, stirring. Add the prunes and figs and simmer for 20 minutes, stirring occasionally, until they are plump, sweet and tender.

Serve a ladleful of sweet risotto in each bowl, and spoon the warm fruits and their cooking juices over. **Serves four**

# sweetened ricotta and baked rhubarb are linked by warm berries melting into a sauce

**main players:**

*1 pound rhubarb, trimmed and washed*

*1 pound fresh ricotta cheese*

*1 pint raspberries or other berries*

**supporting cast:**

*3 tablespoons brown sugar*

*1 tablespoon white sugar*

Heat oven to 350°F. Cut the rhubarb stalks in half.

Place ricotta cheese in a small baking dish and cover with foil. Arrange a layer of rhubarb in another dish and sprinkle with brown sugar and 2 tablespoons of water. Bake both the ricotta and rhubarb for 30 minutes.

Remove the foil from the ricotta, sprinkle with white sugar and bake for another 10 minutes, uncovered, until lightly golden. In the meantime, sprinkle the rhubarb with berries and bake for another 10 minutes until the berries and rhubarb are soft and a syrup has formed.

Cut the ricotta into wedges and divide among serving plates. Top with rhubarb and berries, and a spoonful of cooking juices. **Serves four**

ricotta    rhubarb    berries

# soft, warm Mexican quesadillas filled with a gentle melt of fresh mozzarella cheese and wilted spinach

tortilla

cheese

spinach

**main players:**

*2 large bunches spinach, washed*

*1 mozzarella cheese or 6 bocconcini (small
   mozzarella balls)*

*8 flour tortillas, 7-inch diameter*

**supporting cast:**

*sea salt and freshly ground black pepper*

Roughly chop the spinach, discarding stalks. Stuff it into a large saucepan with 1 cup of water and jam on the lid. Bring to a boil and cook gently for 5 minutes until it wilts to a glossy green mass. Remove, drain and cool. When cool, squeeze the spinach in your hands to wring out excess water. Chop finely and set aside.

Slice the cheese finely and set aside. Heat a nonstick frying pan for 1 minute over a moderate heat. Lay out 4 tortillas and spread each one with a quarter of the spinach, right to the edges. Arrange slices of cheese over the top and sprinkle with salt and pepper. Top with another tortilla and press down gently to flatten.

Place one tortilla sandwich in the hot pan and dry-fry for 2–3 minutes until the cheese just starts to soften. Turn carefully and fry on the other side. Slide out of the pan onto a plate and keep warm while you make the remaining sandwiches. Cut each one into six wedges and serve. **Serves four**

# The best thing about making your own

lunch is that you know where it's been. Why pay good money for a lousy focaccia stacked with oily layers of unrecognizable drabness in a café full of nonentities, when you can stay home for lunch and eat something absolutely gorgeous in the company of stylish, fabulous people such as yourself? Lunch needs a sense of the silly to be successful. Reinvent the ploughman's lunch, the school lunchbox, the office sandwich and the street-stall snacks of Asia. Then mix them all up and forget I said anything. Nobody said lunch had to be sensible. Besides, it's the middle of the day and time to relax. Not you, silly. Your food. It needs to take it easy for a while, take a break from dressing up and working too hard. Food gets stressed too, you know.

# lunch

shrimp

tomato

halloumi

a **new** look at a Greek classic; the acid **freshness** of tomato **shakes** up sweet shrimp and salty cheese

**main players:**

*32 small raw shrimp or 24 medium shrimp*

*6 ripe plum (roma) tomatoes*

*7 ounces halloumi cheese*

**supporting cast:**

*3 tablespoons extra-virgin olive oil*

*2 lemons*

*freshly ground black pepper*

Heat oven to 350°F. Devein the shrimp by inserting a fine bamboo skewer through the back and hooking out any black intestinal tract. Peel them, leaving the tails on. Thread three or four shrimp onto eight skewers and set aside.

Cut the tomatoes in half lengthwise. Arrange them, cut side up, on a baking sheet, brush with a little of the olive oil, and bake for 30 minutes until soft and lightly browned. Juice one lemon and cut the other into quarters.

Cut halloumi into four ½-inch thick sheets. Heat a little of the olive oil in a heavy pan and fry the cheese on one side only until golden. Turn out the cooked cheese onto serving plates.

Brush the shrimp with olive oil and fry quickly in a nonstick pan over a high heat, turning once, until the flesh turns opaque.

Arrange 3 oven-roasted tomato halves on top of each slice of cheese, and lean two skewers of shrimp against the stack. Drizzle with olive oil and lemon juice, and sprinkle with black pepper. Serve with lemon wedges. **Serves four**

a sizzle and a stir – when the tomatoes just burst at their seams, your lunch is ready

**main players:**

*1 pound cleaned squid tubes*

*½ pound cherry tomatoes*

*1 small bunch basil*

**supporting cast:**

*4 anchovy fillets*

*2 tablespoons olive oil*

*freshly ground black pepper*

squid

tomato

basil

Clean and rinse the squid tubes, then slice into rings about ½ inch wide. Drain the anchovy fillets. Wash the tomatoes and shake dry. Pick the leaves off the basil and discard the stems.

Gently warm the olive oil in a frying pan and fry the anchovies until they start to melt. Turn up the heat and add the squid tubes, tossing well for 1–2 minutes until the flesh turns opaque.

Add the tomatoes and toss well, allowing most of the tomatoes to soften and explode, bursting their juices through the sauce. Add most of the basil leaves and the pepper and stir through quickly. Serve piled high on serving plates sprinkled with the remaining basil leaves. Try this on its own, with a green salad, as a pasta sauce, or over soft polenta. **Serves four**

beef

pickles

cheese

a **glamorous** play on the ploughman's lunch – rare roast beef, Cheddar cheese and pickled onions

**main players:**

*14 ounces beef fillet*

*7 ounces Cheddar cheese*

*4 pickled onions*

**supporting cast:**

*3 tablespoons extra-virgin olive oil*

*1 tablespoon white wine vinegar*

*1 teaspoon Dijon mustard*

*sea salt and freshly ground black pepper*

Grill the beef on all sides for around 10 minutes until well-marked on the outside but still rare inside.

Remove from the heat and allow to rest for 30 minutes. Slice the cheese and onions into very thin slices.

To serve, slice the rested beef into ½-inch-thick slices, and season with salt and pepper. Layer the beef and cheese on each plate and top with sliced onions. Fish out any pickling spices from the jar of onions and use them as well.

Whisk the olive oil, vinegar, mustard, salt and pepper in a bowl, and drizzle over the top. (Or beat the mustard into a good quality mayonnaise and serve on the side.)

**Serves four**

artichokes

# earth meets sea in this rustic skewer of artichoke hearts and fresh tuna, scented with bay leaves and drizzled with olive oil

tuna

lemon

**main players:**

*2 x 10-ounce thick tuna steaks*

*12 artichoke hearts in olive oil*

*2 lemons*

**supporting cast:**

*12 bay leaves*

*sea salt and freshly ground black pepper*

Trim the tuna steaks of all blood lines and cut into 24 small cubes, each measuring about 1 inch. Sprinkle with salt and pepper. If the artichoke hearts are on the large side, cut them in half. Reserve the oil they are in.

Thread tuna and artichoke hearts onto eight bamboo skewers, separating them occasionally with the bay leaves. (Make sure you pierce the tuna against the grain, so that it doesn't flake off the skewer.) Cut the lemon into eight wedges and attach a wedge to the end of each skewer; set the remaining wedges aside.

Brush the tuna, artichoke hearts and lemon wedges with some of the oil from the artichoke hearts, or extra olive oil. Heat a large nonstick frying pan, and fry the tuna skewers for 2 minutes on each side, until the fish is slightly crusty but still pink inside.

Brush the extra lemon wedges with oil and quickly fry. Serve tuna sticks with fried lemon wedges and drizzle with a little extra olive oil. **Serves four**

# sizzling shrimp with a cool-as-a-cucumber yogurt dressing

cucumber

yogurt

shrimp

**main players:**

*1 cucumber*

*2 cups plain yogurt*

*12 medium raw shrimp*

**supporting cast:**

*1 teaspoon salt*

*2 garlic cloves, peeled and crushed*

*1 tablespoon white wine vinegar*

*1 tablespoon olive oil, plus extra for frying*

Peel, seed and finely chop the cucumber. Sprinkle it with the salt and leave to drain for an hour or so. In the meantime, place the yogurt in a wrap of two sheets of cheesecloth and hang to drain over a bowl.

After 1 hour, squeeze any excess water from the yogurt and place it in a bowl. Beat in the garlic, vinegar and olive oil. Squeeze excess water from the cucumber and stir into the yogurt.

Devein the shrimp by inserting a fine bamboo skewer through the back and hooking out any black intestinal tract. Peel the shrimp, leaving the tails on. Brush with a little olive oil and broil or sauté quickly until cooked.

To serve, stack shrimp on four serving plates and spoon cucumber and yogurt sauce on top. **Serves four**

# fish

# tomato

# chile

# a tangy Thai dish you can do in the time it takes to cook the rice

**main players:**

*12 ounces canned plum (roma) tomatoes*

*1 tablespoon sweet chile sauce*

*4 fresh snapper fillets, skinned*

**supporting cast:**

*2 tablespoons vegetable oil*

*2 onions, finely chopped*

*2 tablespoons lime juice*

*sea salt and freshly ground black pepper*

*steamed jasmine rice to serve*

Heat the oil in a frying pan and cook the onions for 10 minutes over a moderate heat until soft but still pale. Chop the tomatoes finely, saving all the juices, and add them to the pan with the sweet chile sauce, salt and pepper. Add 1 cup water, cover and cook for 10–15 minutes until the sauce thickens.

When the sauce is ready, slide the fish fillets into the simmering sauce and cook for a few minutes only, until the flesh turns opaque and flakes easily.

Add lime juice to the sauce and taste for a final balance of chile, lime, salt and pepper. Serve with plenty of steamed jasmine rice.

**Serves four**

clams

beans

mint

# a warm Italian salad of fresh baby clams, spiked with mint and served with white beans: the perfect summer lunch

**main players:**

*2 pounds small clams*

*1 pound canned white beans*

*1 small bunch mint*

**supporting cast:**

*4 tablespoons extra-virgin olive oil, plus extra*

   *for drizzling*

*½ cup white wine*

*freshly ground black pepper*

Scrub the clams well. Drain the canned beans and rinse well. Pick the leaves from the mint stalks.

Heat half the olive oil, the white wine and half the mint leaves in a heavy frying pan with a lid. When bubbling, add the clams and cover tightly. Cook over high heat for 2 minutes, then remove the lid. Using tongs, remove all the clams that have opened, then give the pan a big shake and just keep removing the clams as they open. Place the cooked clams in a bowl and cover to keep warm. Throw away any that don't open, as they're not fresh.

When you have picked out all the clams, drain the pan juices through a piece of dampened cheesecloth or a fine sieve into a small bowl. Gently warm the remaining olive oil in a frying pan and add the drained beans, remaining mint and pepper. Add a spoonful or two of the pan juices.

When the beans are heated through, add the clams, toss through once or twice, and divide among four bowls or serve on a large serving platter. Serve warm or at room temperature. Drizzle with oil before serving. **Serves four**

sake

salmon

radish

Japanese minimalist art, **perfectly** steamed salmon with a pinch of grated radish sits in a pool of sweet sake broth

**main players:**

*4 x 7-ounce salmon fillets*

*1 long white radish (daikon)*

*¾ cup sake*

**supporting cast:**

*1 tablespoon instant dashi powder*

*2 tablespoons soy sauce*

*2 tablespoons mirin*

*1 tablespoon sugar*

*sea salt*

Skin salmon and use tweezers to remove any fine bones. Cut a cross into the flesh of each fillet and sprinkle lightly with salt.

Peel the white radish and grate until you have enough to fill 2 tablespoons. Set aside in a sieve to drain. Cut the remaining radish lengthwise into very thin long strips.

Bring plenty of water to a boil in a steamer. Arrange strips of radish on a heatproof plate and place the salmon fillets on top. Pour sake over the salmon, cover with foil and steam for 8–10 minutes until the salmon is just cooked through and flakes easily.

To make the broth, combine instant dashi powder with 1 cup water and bring to a boil. Add the soy, mirin, and sugar and heat, stirring, until the sugar has completely dissolved.

Divide the long strips of radish and salmon between four small Japanese bowls, then pour the broth around each salmon piece.

Squeeze out any excess moisture from the grated radish and arrange a big pinch of it on top of each salmon fillet. Serve with spoons and chopsticks. **Serves four**

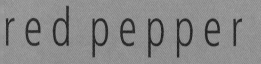

# sardine

# arugula

# red pepper

the **crisp** texture and oily flesh of the sardine plays off **sweet** red pepper and **peppery** arugula leaves

**main players:**

4 red peppers

12 fresh sardines, filleted

7 ounces baby arugula

**supporting cast:**

4 tablespoons extra-virgin olive oil

1 cup dried bread crumbs

1 tablespoon red wine vinegar

1 tablespoon tiny capers, rinsed

sea salt and freshly ground black pepper

Heat oven to 350°F. Rub a little of the olive oil over the skin of the peppers and roast on a baking sheet for 30 minutes until scorched and blistered. Remove from the oven and place in a covered bowl for 10 minutes. Peel off the skins, cut in half and discard the core and seeds but save the juices. Cut the flesh into wide strips and set aside.

Clean and dry the sardines, then brush lightly with a little of the olive oil. Press each side into the bread crumbs. Heat the remaining olive oil in a frying pan and quickly fry the sardines until lightly golden on both sides.

Wash and dry the arugula. Whisk the vinegar and 3 tablespoons of the pepper juices with the capers, salt and pepper, and toss the arugula lightly in the dressing.

Divide the arugula between four serving plates. Top with folds of roasted red pepper and arrange the sardine fillets on top. Spoon any remaining dressing over and serve. **Serves four**

shells of pasta filled with a **quick stir** of warm tomatoes and **fresh** basil – **summer** on a plate

pasta

tomato

basil

**main players:**

6 large ripe tomatoes

1 small bunch basil

20 large pasta shells (conchiglie or lumache)

**supporting cast:**

2 tablespoons extra-virgin olive oil, plus extra

for pasta

2 teaspoons sugar

sea salt and freshly ground black pepper

Dunk the tomatoes in a pan of boiling water for 30 seconds, then peel off the skins, cut in half, squeeze to remove seeds, and chop the remaining flesh.

Heat the olive oil, tomatoes, half the basil leaves, sugar, salt and pepper and cook for about 15 minutes over medium heat until the tomatoes are soft and sweet, and almost soupy.

Cook the pasta shells in plenty of salted, boiling water until tender, but still firm to the bite.

Drain the pasta and toss the shells in a little olive oil to prevent them from sticking. Gently toss pasta shells in the tomato and basil sauce, making sure the sauce slips inside the shells. Add the remaining basil leaves and toss quickly. Divide between four pasta bowls and serve. **Serves four**

# crisp-fried shrimp and fish in a beer batter, served with deep-fried lemon slices

**main players:**

1½ cups flat beer

4 x 5-ounce fresh white fish fillets, such as cod
   or hake

8 medium raw shrimp

**supporting cast:**

1½ cups all-purpose flour

1 teaspoon brown sugar

2 lemons

vegetable oil for deep-frying

sea salt and freshly ground black pepper

To make the batter, mix the flour, sugar, salt and pepper in a large bowl. Add the beer slowly, whisking until smooth and thick. Set aside for 10 minutes.

Trim the fish into portions the size of a large forefinger. Devein the shrimp by inserting a fine bamboo skewer through the back and hooking out any black intestinal tract. Peel them, leaving the tails on.

Slice one lemon as thinly as possible and dry each slice with paper towels. Cut the other lemon into quarters.

Heat the oil until it starts to smoke. Dip the pieces of fish in the batter until well coated and deep-fry until golden. Remove and drain on paper towels. Do the same with the shrimp, and then the lemon slices.

Arrange the fish and shrimp in piles on four serving plates, and top with deep-fried lemon slices and lemon wedges. Serve with a cold glass of beer, of course. **Serves four**

fish

shrimp

beer

# chicken wings marinated in Japanese flavors and broiled until golden

**main players:**

*10 chicken wings*

*2 tablespoons grated fresh ginger*

*3 green onions, finely chopped*

**supporting cast:**

*3 tablespoons sake*

*3 tablespoons soy sauce*

*3 tablespoons mirin*

*1 lemon, quartered*

*sea salt*

*steamed rice to serve*

Cut the tips from the chicken wings. Bend each wing until you can see the joint, then cut through with a sharp knife and trim into 2 neat pieces. Rub each piece with salt.

Mix the grated ginger and most of the green onions with the sake, soy and mirin. Toss the chicken wings in the marinade until well coated, cover with plastic wrap and leave for at least 30 minutes.

Heat the broiler or a cast-iron griddle. Drain the wings, reserving the marinade, and cook on both sides until half cooked, for about 10 minutes. Coat in the marinade once more, then cook for a further 10 minutes, or until golden and tender, turning once or twice. Sprinkle with the remaining green onions and serve with lemon wedges and steamed rice.

**Serves four**

chicken

onion

ginger

Don't let the kitchen get in your way. It's not a relentlessly tidy shrine; a space dedicated solely to the processing of food. It's just a place where violence meets entertainment and comes up with something to eat. Keep it fueled up and ready to service you when you need it. Walk in, fix yourself a drink, open the fridge, start up the stove, and chop an onion. If you can chop an onion, you can cook dinner any time, anywhere, for anyone. If you also own a sharp knife, a fat chopping board, a good pan and an oven that works, then that's about as good as it gets.

The only other thing you need is the food itself. Buy the best, and you'll eat better as well as faster. If you start with great stuff, you need to do very little to make it better. The best thing about staying at home to cook, of course, is that you eat so well. That, and the fact that you don't have to think about putting on enough clothes to appear decently in public.

# dinner

beef

zucchini

red pepper

# grilled beef fillet with Mediterranean vegetables, topped with a dollop of garlicky aïoli

**main players:**

*14 ounces beef fillet, tied with string*

*2 medium zucchini*

*2 red peppers*

**supporting cast:**

*2 garlic cloves, peeled*

*1/2 teaspoon sea salt*

*2 egg yolks*

*1 1/4 cups good, fruity olive oil,*

*plus extra for peppers*

*2 tablespoons lemon juice*

*freshly ground black pepper*

To make the aïoli, crush the garlic and salt together until mushy. Beat in the egg yolks until you have a creamy paste. Add the olive oil really slowly – drip by drip at first, then a little faster – beating constantly, until you have a thickened sauce. Beat in the lemon juice and pepper to taste. Lighten the aïoli if needed, by beating in a little warm water. (You can do all this in the food processor or by hand.) Refrigerate until needed.

Grill the beef on all sides until well-marked but still rare inside, about 8 minutes. Remove it from the heat and allow to rest for 10 minutes.

Cut the zucchini lengthwise into thin strips, and cut each pepper lengthwise into four quarters, discarding the core and seeds. Brush with a little olive oil and broil or fry in a ridged cast-iron griddle on both sides until blistered and soft.

To serve, cut off the string and slice the beef into 1/2-inch-thick slices. Pile the zucchini and red pepper in the center of each plate and top with sliced beef. Add a spoonful of aïoli on top and serve.

**Serves four**

a **sweet** and mushy baked apple becomes a **juicy sauce** for a **simply** cooked pork chop

**main players:**

*4 Granny Smith apples*

*8 sage leaves, chopped*

*4 thick pork loin chops*

**supporting cast:**

*1 cup white wine*

*1 tablespoon butter*

*1 tablespoon extra-virgin olive oil*

*sea salt and freshly ground black pepper*

*Dijon mustard to serve*

Heat oven to 350°F. Core the apples and score the skins to stop them from splitting. Place them on a baking sheet, add the white wine and bake for 45 minutes until the apples are soft.

Heat the butter, oil and sage leaves in a large frying pan. Add the pork chops and cook over moderate heat, not too high, for 8–10 minutes. Season well with salt and pepper.

Turn once, scoop up the cooked sage leaves and place them on top of each chop. Cook the remaining side gently for 5 minutes until tender and just cooked through.

In the meantime, gently remove the apples from their cooking juices, pour the juices into a pan and boil furiously until the liquid is reduced to about $1/2$ cup.

Place a pork chop on each plate, top with a baked apple and spoon the juices over. Serve with Dijon mustard. **Serves four**

pork

sage

apple

# fresh salmon meets creamy avocado and the citrus tang of grapefruit

avocado

grapefruit

salmon

**main players:**

*2 large ripe avocados*

*2 ripe grapefruit, peeled*

*4 x 5-ounce fresh salmon fillets, with skin*

**supporting cast:**

*2 tablespoons lemon juice*

*4 tablespoons extra-virgin olive oil, plus*

*   1 tablespoon extra for frying*

*sea salt and freshly ground black pepper*

Whisk the lemon juice, olive oil, salt and pepper in a large bowl to make a dressing.

Cut an avocado in half lengthwise. Hit the pit with the blade of a large knife, then turn the knife to twist out the pit. Peel off the skin and cut the flesh into chunks, dropping them directly into the dressing. Repeat with the remaining avocado.

Trim any white pith from the grapefruit. Cut into segments and cut the segments in half. Add the grapefruit and any extra juices to the dressing. Toss lightly and chill for 10 minutes or so.

Heat the remaining oil in a heavy pan and cook the salmon, skin-side down, until the skin is crisp and the flesh turns pale pink. Turn and cook on the other side, leaving the salmon soft and pink in the middle.

Place the salmon, skin side up, on serving plates and top with a big spoonful of avocado and grapefruit. Spoon the juices around the salmon and serve. **Serves four**

# chicken

# prosciutto

# peas

tender chicken breast **wrapped** in prosciutto and roasted, served on a bed of **smashed peas**

**main players:**

4 x 5-ounce boneless chicken breasts with

  skin and wing attached

8 thin slices prosciutto

6 cups fresh or frozen peas

**supporting cast:**

2 tablespoons extra-virgin olive oil

2 cups chicken stock or water

1 tablespoon butter

sea salt and freshly ground black pepper

Heat oven to 350°F. Heat the oil in a frying pan until hot. Add the chicken portions, skin side down, and sear each breast until lightly browned on both sides, for about 5 minutes. Remove and drain on paper towels.

Wrap each chicken portion in two slices of prosciutto, securing it with a wooden toothpick if needed. Transfer to an ovenproof dish, add a few spoonfuls of stock or water to the pan, and bake for 10–12 minutes. Remove and allow to rest for 5 minutes before serving.

Cook the peas in the remaining chicken stock or in simmering, salted water for 10 minutes until tender (5 minutes for frozen peas), then remove from the heat and drain into a heatproof bowl, reserving the liquid.

Add the butter to the peas, and roughly mash with a potato masher. Add the cooking liquid back into the peas, spoonful by spoonful, beating with a wooden spoon. Stop when the peas have absorbed enough liquid to be moist. Serve a big dollop of peas in the center of each plate and top with chicken. **Serves four**

# golden grains of fruity couscous served with grilled vegetables and a spicy tomato sauce

**main players:**

*4 red peppers*

*2 x 14-ounce cans chickpeas*

*1 pound couscous*

**supporting cast:**

*8 dried apricots*

*2 tablespoons extra-virgin olive oil*

*14-ounce can plum (roma) tomatoes*

*1/2 teaspoon ground cumin*

*1 tablespoon butter*

*sea salt and freshly ground black pepper*

Soak the apricots in 1 cup of warm water for 30 minutes. Cut each red pepper lengthwise into 3 sections and remove the inner core and seeds. Brush with the olive oil and broil on both sides until well marked.

Purée half the red peppers in a food processor with the tomatoes and their juices, cumin, salt and pepper. Transfer to a saucepan. Drain the chickpeas and rinse well under cold running water. Drain again, add to the sauce, and simmer gently for 10 minutes.

Drain the apricots and cut into slices. Combine with the couscous in a heatproof bowl. Add the butter and 1 2/3 cups boiling water and stir through. Cover and keep warm for 5 minutes while the couscous expands, then fluff it up with a fork.

Spoon the couscous onto a large warmed serving plate and arrange the grilled pepper slices on top. Pour the red pepper sauce over and serve at the table so that everyone can help themselves. **Serves four**

a **cold night** calls for desperate measures and a hearty rice dish that needs a good **bottle of red** as much as you do

**main players:**

*3 Italian pork sausages*

*1¼ cups Arborio rice*

*½ cup good red wine*

**supporting cast:**

*1 tablespoon butter*

*1 onion, finely chopped*

*3 cups hot chicken stock*

*1 tablespoon grated Parmesan cheese, plus*

*extra to serve*

*sea salt and freshly ground black pepper*

Heat a nonstick frying pan. Skin the sausages and pinch small sections of them into the pan. Fry gently until lightly crusty and golden, then drain off any fat, and set aside the sausage meat in a warm place.

Melt the butter in a heavy saucepan, add the onion and cook over moderate heat until it softens. Add the rice and toss until well coated in butter, stirring constantly. Add the red wine and allow it to bubble and be absorbed for 2 minutes, stirring. Add the sausage and stir through.

Add the chicken stock and bring back to a boil. Reduce the heat to very low, cover and cook for 15–20 minutes until the rice has absorbed the stock and is tender, stirring occasionally. Add the Parmesan, stir, taste for salt and pepper, and serve with extra grated Parmesan. **Serves four**

rice    red wine    sausage

# sweet, scorched lamb chops with the flavor of a Cantonese roast meats stall, served with crisp Chinese broccoli

**main players:**

*8 or 12 well-trimmed lamb chops*

*3 tablespoons hoisin sauce*

*1 Chinese broccoli (gai laan)*

**supporting cast:**

*2 tablespoons soy sauce*

*2 tablespoons sugar*

*1 tablespoon rice wine or dry sherry*

*$1/2$ teaspoon five-spice powder*

*$1/2$ teaspoon salt*

*1 teaspoon sesame oil*

For well-trimmed chops, buy racks of lamb and ask the butcher to cut through the bones, or chop through the final linked bone with a Chinese cleaver.

Combine hoisin, soy sauce, sugar, rice wine, five-spice powder and salt in a large bowl and add the lamb chops. Leave to marinate for 1 hour, turning once or twice.

Heat the broiler or barbecue grill. Drain the chops and broil or grill, turning once or twice. The outer meat will scorch as the sugar caramelizes – which is good – but be wary of burning, and remove the chops while the lamb is still pink and tender inside.

Meanwhile, chop the broccoli into 2-inch sections, dividing the stems from the leaves. Cook the stems in simmering, salted water for 2 minutes, then add the leaves and cook for up to 1 minute until they soften. Remove and drain in a colander.

Arrange a neat layer of stems on four warmed dinner plates, and top with leaves. Drizzle the greens with sesame oil, lean 2 or 3 lamb chops against them and serve.

**Serves four**

lamb

hoisin

greens

only **meaty, fresh tuna** can stand up to the slight bitterness of radicchio, the salt factor of bacon and the **sweet tang** of balsamic vinegar

**main players:**

*4 x 9-ounce tuna steaks*

*2 heads radicchio*

*8 thin slices bacon or pancetta*

**supporting cast:**

*1 tablespoon extra-virgin olive oil, plus 2*

   *tablespoons extra to serve*

*2 tablespoons balsamic vinegar, plus 2*

   *tablespoons extra to serve*

Heat a large nonstick frying pan and cook the bacon until crisp on both sides. Add the radicchio and toss over high heat. Add the balsamic vinegar and keep tossing until the radicchio starts to wilt.

Divide the wilted radicchio and most of the bacon between four warmed dinner plates. Place the tuna steaks on top, and arrange a little bacon on top of the tuna. Drizzle with any cooking juices from the pan, and the extra olive oil and balsamic vinegar and serve. **Serves four**

Brush the tuna lightly with olive oil and broil or sauté on one side for 4 minutes, and on the other side for 2–3 minutes until the outside becomes slightly crusty but the inside is still rare.

Cut out the radicchio cores, separate the leaves and wash and dry them. If the leaves are very large, tear them in half lengthwise. Cut the bacon slices in half.

tuna

radicchio

bacon

a fast "sauerkraut" of cabbage **spiked** with caraway seeds lies beneath **gently poached** salmon

**main players:**

*4 x 7-ounce fillets fresh salmon*

*1/2 medium white cabbage, around 2*
*   pounds, cored and finely shredded*

*10 small potatoes*

**supporting cast:**

*sea salt*

*1 tablespoon butter*

*3/4 cup white wine*

*1 tablespoon white wine vinegar*

*2 teaspoons caraway seeds*

Remove any skin and bones from the salmon and set aside.

Cook the potatoes (peeled or unpeeled, it's your call) in simmering, salted water for 15 minutes until tender.

Cook the cabbage in simmering, salted water for 10 minutes until still fairly crunchy, then drain well.

Melt the butter in a frying pan, add the wine and bring to a boil. Add the drained cabbage and toss well. Arrange the salmon fillets on top, cover tightly, and cook over gentle heat for about 10 minutes until the cabbage is tender and the salmon is cooked but still pink and moist in the center.

Gently remove the salmon fillets and keep warm. Add the vinegar and half the caraway seeds to the cabbage and toss well for 1 minute. Arrange a heap of cabbage on four warmed dinner plates and top each with a salmon fillet. Drain the potatoes, cut in half and tuck them around the salmon. Sprinkle with the remaining caraway seeds and serve. **Serves four**

salmon

cabbage

potato

prawns

chile

ginger

# messy, juicy and downright delicious Singaporean chile prawns in a lush, spicy tomato sauce

**main players:**

*12 large raw prawns*

*2-inch piece of ginger, peeled*

*2 tablespoons sweet chile sauce*

**supporting cast:**

*2 tablespoons vegetable oil*

*1 cup hot chicken stock*

*4 tablespoons tomato ketchup*

*1 tablespoon soy sauce*

*2 teaspoons sugar*

*1/2 teaspoon sea salt*

*1 heaping teaspoon cornstarch, blended*
  *with 1 tablespoon cold water*

Devein prawns by inserting a wooden bamboo skewer through their backs and hooking out the thin, black vein. Do not peel. Thinly slice the ginger and cut each slice into thin matchsticks.

Heat the oil in a wok or frying pan and fry the ginger for 30 seconds over a high heat. Add the prawns and cook for a minute or two. Remove the prawns and ginger and set aside.

To the remaining oil in the wok, add the chile sauce, chicken stock, tomato sauce, soy sauce, sugar and salt, and stir well to mix. Add the cornstarch paste, bring to a boil and stir for 1 minute until the sauce thickens.

Return the cooked prawns and ginger to the wok and toss well for a couple of minutes to heat through until well coated in the sauce. Serve with plenty of noodles, or jasmine rice for mopping up the juices.

**Serves four**

# veal

# cheese

# tomato

a last-minute melt of **fresh** cheese and tomato
with **crisply crumbed** tender veal

**main players:**

*4 large or 8 small veal cutlets, on the bone*

*1 mozzarella or 6 bocconcini (small*
*mozzarella balls)*

*4 small ripe tomatoes*

**supporting cast:**

*3 tablespoons all-purpose flour*

*2 eggs*

*1 cup dried bread crumbs*

*1 tablespoon olive oil*

*1 tablespoon butter*

*sea salt and freshly ground black pepper*

Place each veal cutlet on a sheet of plastic wrap and cover with another sheet of plastic wrap. Use a meat mallet, or some other heavy murder weapon, to flatten the meat to a uniform ½ inch.

Sift the flour into a bowl and season with salt and pepper. Beat the eggs in a shallow bowl. Place the bread crumbs in a third bowl.

Slice the mozzarella and tomatoes and arrange in slightly overlapping layers on a foil-covered baking sheet. Sprinkle with salt and pepper.

Heat the broiler, and have four plates ready.

Heat the oil and butter in a heavy-bottomed frying pan. Dip each veal cutlet first in the flour, then the egg, then the bread crumbs, and fry on both sides over a moderate heat until golden. Place the cheese and tomatoes under the broiler (or in a hot oven) for a few minutes until the cheese starts to melt.

Drain the cutlets on paper towels, and arrange on each plate with the tomatoes and cheese. **Serves four**

dried **pasta** from Italy **comes to life** with green peas and that other **old faithful** – canned tuna

**main players:**

*1 pound dried tortellini*

*2 cups fresh or frozen peas*

*1 cup canned tuna in olive oil*

**supporting cast:**

*sea salt and freshly ground black pepper*

Cook the tortellini in a large pot of simmering, salted water, according to the package instructions, then drain. Cook the peas in simmering, salted water until tender, and drain.

Combine the drained tortellini, peas, canned tuna with its olive oil, salt and pepper in a frying pan and heat through, tossing gently.

Divide between four warmed plates and serve. **Serves four**

tortellini

peas

tuna

You know you don't need it, but you want it. You deserve it. Damn it, you have a right to it. Just make it fresh, fruity, light and bright, and jump into it. Go beyond cream and ice cream as additives, and think sweet syrups, a handful of toasted nuts and tangy yogurt instead. That way, you can have three helpings. Cream is just a habit you get into, like adding salt. It can mask the flavors until they die of creaminess. Chocolate, on the other hand, is a fine and wonderful thing that comes somewhere very soon after global peace on the list of things the world cannot do without. The trick is to go for sweet things that contribute more than just sugar to our lives. Toffeed figs. A mousse with the bittersweetness of espresso. Fresh cheese drizzled with honey. Biscotti dipped into liqueur. Little sweets to serve with mint tea. These are desserts that don't just sit there smiling sweetly, they do something.

# dessert

are these cute or what? little éclairs you build yourself from ladyfingers, fruity ice cream and berries

**main players:**

*14 ounces berry ice cream*

*8 thin ladyfinger cookies*

*1 pint strawberries, raspberries or blueberries*

Take the ice cream from the freezer and leave to soften for 5 minutes. Arrange a ladyfinger on each plate.

Wash the strawberries, if using, and pull out and discard the stems. Cut them in half lengthwise. Select the best-looking of the other berries, but don't wash them or they'll get soggy.

Place two scoops of ice cream on each bottom cookie, and tuck in 3 or 4 berries.

Top with the remaining cookies and push down gently. Scatter the remaining berries around each plate and serve immediately, don't waste any time. **Serves four**

ice cream          cookies          berries

# toffeed figs topped with tangy yogurt and toasted walnuts, done in seconds

**main players:**

*2 tablespoons walnut pieces*

*6 large ripe figs, washed and dried*

*3/4 cup plain yogurt*

**supporting cast:**

*1 tablespoon brown sugar*

Heat a dry frying pan and lightly toast the walnuts for 1–2 minutes. Remove from the pan and crush lightly.

Heat the broiler until really hot. Cut the figs in half lengthwise and sprinkle with sugar.

Broil the figs for 2–3 minutes until the sugar has melted and glazed and the figs are warm. Arrange 3 fig halves on each plate. Top with a dollop of yogurt and a sprinkling of crushed walnuts. **Serves four**

walnut

fig

yogurt

coffee

# a rich espresso mousse that combines the well-matched flavors of coffee, chocolate and rum

**main players:**

*6 ounces unsweetened chocolate*

*2 tablespoons brewed espresso, plus 1*

  *tablespoon ground beans for sprinkling*

*1 teaspoon rum or brandy*

**supporting cast:**

*4 eggs*

Chop the chocolate into small pieces. Mix the chocolate with the brewed coffee in a bowl over a pan of barely simmering water, stirring until melted and smooth. Remove from the heat and allow to cool a little.

Separate the eggs, keeping the yolks in a small bowl and the whites in a large one.

Beat one egg yolk at a time into the cooled chocolate mixture, until they have all been incorporated. Add the rum and stir well.

Beat the egg whites until they form soft white peaks which are not too stiff.

Stir a large spoonful of egg white into the chocolate mixture to lighten it, then pour all the chocolate mixture into the egg whites and fold gently until mixed.

Spoon into individual pots or coffee cups and chill for 1–2 hours until firm. To serve, sprinkle with a little ground coffee.

**Serves six**

rum

chocolate

light **creamy** ricotta, drizzled
with honey and **crunchy** pine nuts

**main players:**

*1 pound fresh ricotta cheese*

*4 tablespoons wild honey*

*2 tablespoons pine nuts*

Toast the pine nuts in a dry frying pan until lightly golden.

Place the ricotta on a serving plate. Dip a spoon in a cup of hot water, shake dry, then dip it into the honey and drizzle honey over the ricotta.

Sprinkle with toasted pine nuts, and serve with spoons. **Serves four**

If you feel the need to do something more complicated (yeah, right), bake the ricotta in the oven according to the method described on page 27. Serve it warm, drizzled with honey and pine nuts. Or make the drunken prunes on page 78 and pour them over the top.

ricotta

honey

pine nuts

# a little glass of sweet mint tea, with dainty sweets on the side

**main players:**

*1¹/₂ cups walnut pieces*

*5 ounces dates, pitted*

*1 small bunch fresh mint*

**supporting cast:**

*1 tablespoon Chinese green tea leaves*

*sugar to taste*

*confectioner's sugar for dusting*

Lightly toast the walnuts in a dry frying pan until they smell fragrant.

Place the dates and walnuts in the food processor and blend until they form a paste. If the paste is a little dry, add a teaspoon of water, rose water or liqueur. Press a teaspoon of the mixture into the palm of your hand, roll into a ball and set down on a small tray. Continue until the mixture is finished, making 12 balls, and refrigerate until needed.

To make the mint tea, place the tea leaves in a pot and top with boiling water, then strain off the water and discard the tea leaves. Add more boiling water, a handful of fresh mint leaves, and a teaspoon of sugar per person. Stir, then strain into small heatproof glasses (place a teaspoon in the glass as you pour to avoid cracking).

Arrange each glass on a serving plate with a few sprigs of mint. Dust the sweets with confectioner's sugar through a sieve and arrange 3 on each plate. **Serves four**

mint

walnuts

dates

# crisp fried wonton wrappers layer ripe mango and creamy yogurt

**main players:**

*12 small square wonton wrappers*

*2 ripe mangoes*

*1 cup plain yogurt*

**supporting cast:**

*vegetable oil for deep-frying*

*confectioner's sugar for dusting*

Heat the oil in a small frying pan and deep-fry the wonton wrappers until crisp and golden. Drain on a cooling rack and dust with confectioner's sugar through a sieve.

Peel the mangoes and cut each one into thick slices, working around the pit. Squeeze the juices from the mango flesh attached to the pit into the yogurt and stir well.

Place 1 wonton wrapper on each plate and top with a slice of mango. Drizzle with some of the yogurt, top with another wonton wrapper, more mango and more yogurt, finishing with a final wonton wrapper. Dust a little confectioner's sugar on top and serve immediately.

**Serves four**

wonton

mango

yogurt

watermelon

rose water

petals

pretty pink **granita**, an icy slush made **glamorous** with floating rose petals

**main players:**

1 1/4 pounds watermelon flesh,

without rind or seeds (reserve a few

seeds for garnish)

1 teaspoon rose water syrup

pink rose petals for serving

**supporting cast:**

1/2 cup sugar

Combine the sugar with 1/2 cup water in a small pan and bring to a boil, stirring until the sugar has dissolved. Remove from the heat and let cool.

Purée the watermelon flesh in a blender to give about 2 cups of liquid.

Combine the watermelon purée, rose water and cooled sugar syrup, and pour the

mixture into a plastic container and place in the freezer.

Leave for 30–60 minutes – depending on the strength of your freezer – until it starts to freeze around the edges. Remove and stir well, breaking up the ice crystals, scraping the hard bits from the side. Return to the freezer and repeat the process every 30 minutes, for 3 or 4 times. The mixture will become increasingly thick and almost gluey, with very fine crystals.

Rinse the rose petals to remove any trace of chemicals and gently pat dry. Divide the granita between four small glasses or glass dishes, scatter with rose petals and a few reserved watermelon seeds and serve.

**Serves four**

Rose water is available from supermarkets and Middle Eastern stores.

grab a spoon and dig in to **plump and potent** drunken prunes, served on a mound of **must-have** mascarpone

espresso

prunes

mascarpone

**main players:**

*2 tablespoons ground espresso beans*

*1 pound large dried prunes, pitted*

*1 pound mascarpone cheese*

**supporting cast:**

*1 cup sugar*

*3 tablespoons brandy or Cognac*

Pour $1/2$ cup of boiling water over the ground espresso and let sit a few minutes, then strain, discarding the grounds.

Heat the coffee, sugar, brandy and 1 cup water in a saucepan and boil for 1 minute. Reduce the heat, add the prunes and cook at a low simmer for 20 minutes, stirring occasionally, until the prunes soften and plump up and the liquid reduces to a syrupy consistency. If the liquid isn't very syrupy, bring to a boil and allow to reduce for a minute or two, watching carefully.

Remove from the heat and set aside, leaving the prunes in the liquid until ready to serve.

Place a big dollop of mascarpone in the center of each plate and arrange a few of the prunes on top. Drizzle with the syrup and serve. **Serves four**

# very daring – a sort of kid's-drink-turned-cocktail-turned-dessert served in martini glasses – but very refreshing

**main players:**

*1 pound sorbet, such as berry or lemon*

*1 pint fresh berries, such as raspberries*

*1 cup Champagne – drink the rest*

Chill four martini glasses until cold.

Arrange one or two scoops of sorbet in each one, depending on the size of glass, and scatter the sorbet with berries.

Very slowly and carefully – or it will fizz up too much – pour the Champagne on top until the sorbet is almost submerged. Serve immediately. **Serves four**

sorbet

champagne          berries

# oooh, sexy. The perfect pear-shaped pear, generously draped with rich, dark chocolate

**main players:**

*6 Bosc or Bartlett pears*

*3 1/2 ounces unsweetened chocolate*

*1 cup heavy cream*

**supporting cast:**

*5 cups sparkling wine or water*

*2 cups white sugar*

*1/3 cup brown sugar*

*2 tablespoons butter, diced*

Combine the sparkling wine or water and white sugar in a saucepan and bring to a boil, stirring. Wash the pears, but do not peel them. Place them in the syrup and simmer gently for 20–30 minutes, until tender to the touch. Allow the pears to cool in the syrup.

Finely chop the chocolate.

Combine the cream, brown sugar and butter in a small pan and heat, stirring, until the sugar has dissolved and the sauce is smooth. Remove from the heat, add the chopped chocolate and stir well until completely smooth.

Drain the pears well and place one pear in the center of a shallow soup plate. Spoon the hot chocolate sauce over until the whole pear, including the stem, is completely coated. Repeat for the other pears. Serve immediately. **Serves six**

pear

chocolate

cream

oven-roasted peaches – as warm as if taken straight from the sunshine – served with a nutty liqueur and crisp biscuits for dipping

**main players:**

*4 large ripe but firm freestone peaches*

*1 1/2 cups Italian Nocello or Frangelico liqueur*

*12 small biscotti or amaretti cookies*

Heat the oven to 350°F. Cut a small slit around the circumference of each peach and place on a baking sheet. Add a spoonful or 2 of water to the pan and bake for 30 minutes – slightly less for smaller peaches – until they are soft to the touch.

Carefully remove, without bruising, and leave to cool for 10 minutes.

Your choice now is to either leave the peaches looking rustic with their skins on, or to peel them off, which reveals their rosy shoulders. Your call.

Drizzle a little of the liqueur over each peach. Serve one peach per person on a dinner plate, next to a small glass of the liqueur, and a few biscotti for dipping.

**Serves four**

peach      liqueur      biscotti

forget tiramisu – the world has **moved on**, to fresh berries, mascarpone and **melting** ladyfingers

**main players:**

*1 pint strawberries*

*1 pound mascarpone cheese*

*1 pound ladyfinger cookies*

**supporting cast:**

*2 eggs*

*3 tablespoons sugar*

*2 tablespoons brandy or Italian liqueur*

*1/2 cup milk*

Wash the strawberries, remove the stem and cut in half lengthwise. Separate the eggs. Using a wooden spoon, beat the mascarpone with the sugar, egg yolks, and half the brandy or liqueur. In a separate bowl, whisk the egg whites until stiff and peaky, then gently fold them into the cheese mixture.

Combine the remaining brandy or liqueur and milk in a saucer and dip each cookie into the mixture. Use them to line the base of an 8-inch square cake pan, breaking up the biscuits to fill in the corners as necessary.

Cover the cookies with half the cheese mixture, then top with a layer of strawberries. Arrange another layer of soaked cookies on top, another layer of cheese and a final layer of strawberries.

Chill for 4 hours, then serve in big, generous, sloppy spoonfuls. **Serves four**

berries

mascarpone

cookies

If you wouldn't eat it on a plate, don't turn it into a soup. Soup is just food you eat with a spoon, after all. Break the rules. Open the cupboard. Liberate soup from the food police and tailor each bowl to suit: thick, thin, hot, cold. Add a handful of golden bread crumbs, crisp bacon, melting cheese on toast, black olives, sautéed mushrooms, a spoonful of pesto or chile jam. Forget anything you may have heard about soup being a first course. Soup can definitely be the main event. You don't even need a freezer full of stock. Cook a few leeks and carrots in a little butter and add boiling water for instant soup. Or just add water to a couple of chicken pieces and cook until it smells like soup (because it is soup). You can live on soup, if you're clever enough. Or if you don't have any knives and forks.

# soup

# sweet potato

# bacon

# onion

smooth and **luscious** with a deep, mellow flavor, this is **perfect** for a cold winter night and plenty of hot toast

**main players:**

1¹/₂ pounds sweet potatoes

8 thin slices bacon

2 onions, finely chopped

**supporting cast:**

1 tablespoon extra-virgin olive oil

2 bay leaves

5 cups chicken stock

¹/₂ teaspoon freshly grated nutmeg

sea salt and freshly ground black pepper

Heat the oven to 350°F. Cut the sweet potatoes in half lengthwise, rub with the olive oil and bake, cut side down, for 1 hour until tender. Allow to cool, then scoop the flesh out of the skins and discard the skins.

Arrange the bacon on a foil-covered baking sheet and broil or fry in a nonstick frying pan until super crisp. Remove and drain on paper towels, then crumble into small pieces. Cook the onions in the bacon fat or in 1 tablespoon of olive oil over moderate heat for 5 minutes until they start to soften.

Add the sweet potato flesh, bay leaves, chicken stock, nutmeg, salt and pepper and bring to a boil, stirring. Simmer for 15 minutes, stirring occasionally. If it's too lumpy for your taste, remove the bay leaves and purée the soup in the food processor, otherwise leave it alone. Serve in warmed soup bowls, topped with crumbled crisp bacon. **Serves four**

# hearty, rustic and homely – these words give you clues that this dish will look pretty ordinary, but taste great

**main players:**

*1/2 medium white cabbage*

*14 ounces canned white beans*

*4 good quality pork sausages*

**supporting cast:**

*2 onions*

*1 tablespoon butter*

*1 tablespoon extra-virgin olive oil*

*sea salt and freshly ground black pepper*

*Dijon mustard to serve*

Thinly slice the onions. Discard the core and outer leaves of the cabbage and thinly slice the rest. Melt the butter and oil in a large frying pan, add the onions and cook for 15 minutes over low heat until golden. Add the cabbage and cook for 5 minutes.

Add 6 cups of boiling water, salt and pepper, and cook over low heat for 20 minutes, stirring occasionally. Add the beans and cook for another 10 minutes, then taste for salt and pepper.

Meanwhile, prick the sausages and broil until browned. Divide the soup among four shallow soup bowls, top each with a grilled sausage and serve with a pot of Dijon mustard that can be added at the table. Or cut the sausages in thick slices, arrange them in a ring in the center of each bowl, and pour the soup over. **Serves four**

cabbage

sausage

white beans

# the nicest and fastest way to eat mussels – cook them in cider or Champagne, and serve with a touch of cream

**main players:**

*3¹/2 pounds mussels*

*1 cup dry cider or Champagne*

*¹/2 cup light cream*

**supporting cast:**

*1 teaspoon black peppercorns*

Scrub the mussels well, tugging off the little beards. Discard any that are cracked or stay open when you tap them.

Bring the cider and peppercorns to a boil in a large pan with a lid. Add the mussels, cover tightly and quickly bring to a boil.

Give the pan a big shake after 1 minute and use tongs to take out any mussels that have opened. Put these in a large bowl.

Return the lid for another minute and repeat the process until you have removed all the opened mussels. Throw out any that do not open.

Divide the mussels between four warmed soup plates. Strain the cooking liquids through a cheesecloth-lined sieve into a bowl, then put it back in the pan.

Add the cream and heat through, stirring, and then pour the broth over the top.
**Serves four**

mussels    cider    cream

red pepper

# a smooth, ruby red purée with a fresh zippy flavor and a suggestion of spice

tomato

olive

**main players:**

6 red peppers

12 ounces canned plum (roma) tomatoes

20 tiny black olives, pitted, or 2 tablespoons
   tapenade, plus 4 olives, to serve

**supporting cast:**

1/2 teaspoon ground cumin

1/2 teaspoon cayenne pepper

6 cups chicken stock

1 tablespoon extra-virgin olive oil

sea salt and freshly ground black pepper

Heat oven to 400°F. Roast the red peppers on a baking sheet for about 30 minutes until scorched and blistered. Transfer to a covered bowl for 10 minutes until cool enough to handle, then discard the cores and peel off the skins, catching the seeds and juices in the bowl. Strain out the seeds and keep the juices.

Combine the red peppers with the cooking juices, tomatoes, cumin, cayenne pepper, salt and pepper in the food processor and blend until smooth but without over-blending.

Combine the red pepper mixture with the chicken stock and heat to a high simmer. If using black olives, finely chop, mash or purée them and mix with the olive oil.

Taste the soup for salt, pepper and spices, then ladle into soup bowls. Add a spoonful of olive purée or tapenade to each bowl and serve topped with a whole olive.

**Serves four**

tomato

leek

fish

# splash around in a Mediterranean tidepool
of rich tomatoey seafood

**main players:**

*3 tomatoes*

*3 leeks*

*1 pound fresh white fish fillets, such as*

  *cod, hake, halibut or monkfish*

**supporting cast:**

*1 tablespoon butter*

*1 tablespoon extra-virgin olive oil*

*2 tablespoons tomato paste*

*6 cups fish stock or water*

*1 large pinch saffron threads*

*sea salt and freshly ground black pepper*

Cut the tomatoes in half and squeeze out the seeds, then cut the flesh into small cubes. Trim the leeks and thinly slice the white part. Rinse in cold water and drain.

Melt the butter and oil in a frying pan over medium heat, add the leeks and cook until they are soft, about 20 minutes. Add the tomatoes, tomato paste, fish stock, salt and pepper, and stir well. Grind the saffron threads with the back of a wooden spoon in a few drops of warm water. Add the saffron to the pan, stirring. Simmer for 10 minutes.

Cut the fish into bite-size chunks, removing any skin or bones. Slip the fish into the broth and simmer for 5 minutes, until just cooked. Taste for salt and pepper and adjust accordingly.

Use a slotted spoon to divide the leeks and fish among four soup bowls, then pour the broth over. **Serves four**

# gentle Chinese flavors in a bowl: sweet corn plays with sweet crab in a velvety, comforting dish

corn

crab

onion

**main players:**

*2 ears corn*

*6 ounces fresh crab meat*

*2 green onions, thinly sliced*

**supporting cast:**

*6 cups chicken stock*

*1 teaspoon cornstarch*

*sea salt*

*1 egg*

Peel the husks from the corn and cook the corn in simmering salted water for 10 minutes until tender. Cool, then scrape off the kernels with a sharp knife.

Bring the chicken stock to a boil in a saucepan, then reduce to a simmer. Add the crab and corn kernels and cook for 2 minutes, stirring. Combine the cornstarch with 1 tablespoon cold water. Add salt to taste, then stir in the cornstarch paste and bring back to a boil, stirring.

Beat the egg lightly and pour it in a steady stream through the tines of a fork into the soup, whisking lightly so it forms long strands. The soup should be creamy, with a velvety texture and sweet taste.

Pour the soup into warmed Chinese soup bowls and sprinkle with the sliced green onions. **Serves four**

miso

shrimp

mushroom

# light but full of flavor, this versatile Japanese soup could be breakfast, lunch or on the side at the dinner table

**main players:**

*3 tablespoons red miso paste*

*12 small or 6 medium raw shrimp*

*12 oyster mushrooms*

**supporting cast:**

*3 tablespoons instant dashi powder*

*2 tablespoons mirin*

*2 tablespoons light soy sauce*

Combine the instant dashi with 4 cups water and heat until just below boiling point. Add the mirin and soy sauce, stirring.

Remove 4 tablespoons of the broth and let it cool for a minute or two. Whisk it into the miso paste, then pour the miso liquid very slowly back into the hot dashi broth, stirring constantly until well blended. Do not allow it to boil.

Devein the prawns by hooking out the small intestinal tract along the back of each with a fine bamboo skewer. Peel the prawns, leaving the tail intact. Wipe the mushrooms clean with a damp cloth, and cut in half lengthwise, if large.

Add the prawns to the broth and cook for 3–4 minutes until they turn opaque. Add the mushrooms and cook for a further minute.

Divide the broth, prawns and mushrooms between four Japanese soup bowls and serve with chopsticks and china spoons.
**Serves four**

You will find miso paste, a fermented paste made from soy beans, in larger supermarkets, or in the refrigerated section at Japanese food stores or health food stores.

# lentils

# potato

# onion

soup

it's down-home and **hungry** time, with a hearty bowl of lentils simmered with **spices** and potato

**main players:**

2 potatoes

2 onions

1¹/2 cups small brown or green lentils

**supporting cast:**

1 tablespoon butter

1 tablespoon vegetable oil

14 ounces canned plum (roma) tomatoes,

   chopped

¹/2 teaspoon ground cumin

¹/2 teaspoon ground coriander

¹/2 teaspoon cayenne pepper

sea salt and freshly ground black pepper

Peel and finely chop the potatoes and onions. Melt the butter and oil in a frying pan, add the onions and cook for 15 minutes until the onions are soft.

Add the potatoes, lentils and 2 quarts boiling water and return to a boil, skimming off any froth if necessary. Reduce the heat, add the tomatoes, cumin, coriander, cayenne, salt and pepper, and stir well.

Simmer, partly covered, for 1 hour until the potatoes are cooked and the lentils are tender, stirring occasionally.

Taste for spices and adjust accordingly. Spoon into four warmed soup bowls and serve. **Serves four**

# a chilled summer purée that really acts as a kind of exquisitely refreshing cocktail

cucumber

yogurt

mint

**main players:**

*2 cucumbers*

*2 cups plain yogurt*

*1 small bunch mint*

**supporting cast:**

*2 cups chicken stock*

*1 teaspoon paprika*

*sea salt and freshly ground black pepper*

Peel, seed and coarsely chop the cucumber, reserving 1 tablespoon to use as a garnish. Place the cucumber in a food processor, add the yogurt and mint and process until smooth and creamy.

Add the chicken stock, paprika, salt and pepper and process again to mix. Pour into a jug or bowl and refrigerate for several hours.

Serve the soup in small bowls or in cocktail glasses, and top with an ice cube or two and the reserved cucumber. **Serves four**

# bread

# tomato

# garlic

a soup that's really a salad: **sourdough** bread, rich, ripe tomatoes and your **fruitiest** olive oil

**main players:**

*12 ounces stale sourdough bread*

*1 pound ripe tomatoes*

*2 garlic cloves, peeled*

**supporting cast:**

*½ cup extra-virgin olive oil, plus extra*

   *to serve*

*5 cups chicken stock*

*1 small bunch basil*

*sea salt and freshly ground black pepper*

Remove crusts from the bread, thickly slice and cut into ¾-inch cubes. Coarsely chop the tomatoes, and smash the garlic with the side of a knife until flattened.

Heat the olive oil and garlic in a heavy saucepan. When hot, add the tomatoes and cook, stirring, for 5 minutes.

Add the chicken stock gradually, stirring, and bring to a boil. When the mixture is bubbling, add the stale bread cubes, salt and pepper, and cook, stirring, for another 5 minutes. Toss in a handful of fresh basil leaves and stir them through.

Cover and simmer over very low heat for 20–30 minutes. Stir every now and then, squashing some of the bread into the soup with a potato masher or the back of a wooden spoon.

Remove from the heat and leave to cool for a while. Serve just warm, drizzled with extra olive oil. **Serves four**

Three things you should never find in a salad: alfalfa sprouts, grated carrot and banana. Three things you should always find in a salad: freshness, crispness, contrast. Salad isn't lettuce. It's just like a normal meal, only it's younger, smarter, dressier, and more exciting to eat. Great salads also come in bottles. You want fruity extra-virgin olive oil, and vinegar with attitude – balsamic, Champagne, sherry, walnut, or rice wine. Salads can be hot or cold, exotic or everyday. Warm salads have time to mingle and get to know each other, and you have time to do what you want instead of rushing to the table. Salads can be made from take-out chicken, pasta, tuna, beef, sausages, roasted veggies and anything in the bottom of the fridge as long as it is sparkling fresh. And as long as it isn't alfalfa sprouts, grated carrot or banana.

# salad

# chicken

# cucumber

# celery

 salad

# a crisp and crunchy plateful
## of chicken and vegetables

**main players:**

*2 boneless chicken breasts*

*1 large cucumber*

*3 celery stalks*

**supporting cast:**

*8 dried shiitake mushrooms*

*sea salt*

*2 tablespoons soy sauce*

*2 tablespoons rice wine vinegar or white wine*

  *vinegar*

*1 tablespoon sesame oil*

Soak the dried mushrooms in a bowl of warm water for 30 minutes, then rinse well. Trim the stems off, squeeze dry and thinly slice.

Poach the chicken breasts in a pan of simmering, salted water for 20 minutes, until cooked through. Drain, remove the skin and thinly slice.

Peel the cucumber and cut it in half lengthwise. Scoop out and discard the seeds and cut the flesh into long matchsticks, or peel into long strips with a vegetable peeler. Thinly slice the celery on the diagonal.

Mix the soy sauce, vinegar and sesame oil in a bowl and lightly toss the chicken, mushrooms, cucumber and celery in the dressing. Serve in bowls with chopsticks.
**Serves four**

a combination of **tangy Thai** flavors that practically jumps off the plate with freshness

**main players:**

*2 boneless chicken breasts*

*1 small bunch mint*

*4 tablespoons lime juice*

**supporting cast:**

*1 tablespoon vegetable oil*

*1 teaspoon white or palm sugar*

*2 tablespoons Thai fish sauce (nam pla)*

*1/2 teaspoon chile powder*

chicken

mint

lime

Rub the chicken breasts with oil and broil or sauté on both sides for about 15 minutes, until tender and cooked through. Allow to rest.

Pick the mint leaves from the stalks and finely chop half, leaving the rest whole.

Stir the lime juice and sugar with the fish sauce, until the sugar dissolves. Remove the skin from the chicken and thinly slice the breast on the diagonal.

Toss the chicken, chopped mint and chile powder in the dressing, pile high on a serving plate, scatter with the whole leaves and serve. **Serves four**

fresh fish mixed with **ripe** tomatoes and piquant leaves screams **sunny** holidays by the Mediterranean

**main players:**

1 pound fresh fish fillets, such as cod

or hake

3 ripe tomatoes

7 ounces baby arugula or other small green

leaves

**supporting cast:**

1 cup white wine

2 bay leaves

1 lemon

2 tablespoons small black olives

1 tablespoon tiny capers, rinsed

4 tablespoons extra-virgin olive oil

sea salt and freshly ground black pepper

Combine the white wine and bay leaves with 2 cups water and bring to a boil. Reduce the heat to a gentle simmer and add the cod. Simmer for 5 minutes until just cooked, then remove and cool.

Flake the fish into bite-size pieces using your fingers or a knife.

Cut the tomatoes in half and squeeze out and discard the seeds and juice. Cut the flesh into small dice.

Wash and dry the arugula. Juice the lemon.

Combine the arugula, tomatoes, olives and capers in a large bowl. Mix the olive oil with 2 tablespoons of the lemon juice, salt and pepper, and toss the salad lightly in the dressing. Add the flaked fish, lightly toss, and divide between four plates.

**Serves four**

cod

tomato

arugula

# crisp, thin fennel and torn leaves mix with buttery curls of Parmesan to make every mouthful an explosion

**main players:**

*2 fennel bulbs*

*1 head radicchio*

*1 large bunch baby arugula*

**supporting cast:**

*1 small wedge Parmesan cheese*

*1 lemon*

*4 tablespoons extra-virgin olive oil*

*sea salt and freshly ground black pepper*

Wash and trim the fennel, and slice very thinly. Remove the outer leaves of radicchio, and wash and slice the heart into very thin strips. Wash and dry the arugula.

Place the fennel and the salad leaves in a large bowl. Use a vegetable peeler to peel off thin curls of Parmesan, letting them drop onto a sheet of paper.

Squeeze 2 tablespoons of juice from the lemon and whisk it with the olive oil, salt and pepper to make a dressing. Pour the dressing over the salad and toss well. To serve, pile high in the center of each plate. Sprinkle the Parmesan curls over each salad. **Serves four**

arugula

fennel

radicchio

egg

bacon

greens

# thinly sliced omelet links crisp matchsticks of bacon with curly endive

**main players:**

*3 large eggs*

*4 slices bacon*

*1 bunch curly endive (frisée)*

**supporting cast:**

*1 tablespoon vegetable oil*

*3 tablespoons extra-virgin olive oil*

*1 tablespoon white wine vinegar*

*sea salt and freshly ground black pepper*

Beat the eggs together in a small bowl.

Cut the bacon into thick matchsticks and fry in a nonstick frying pan until crisp. Drain the bacon on paper towels and set aside in a warm place.

Separate the leaves of the curly endive, wash well and dry. Cut off any stems.

Heat the vegetable oil in a wok or frying pan, tipping the pan to oil the entire surface. Pour the eggs into the pan and roll the pan around to coat the maximum surface possible with egg.

Move the pan around over the heat while the egg is cooking, until it is firm and no liquid remains. Place a large plate on top, and tip the pan upside down so that the omelet falls onto the plate (with luck).

Sprinkle the omelet with salt and pepper, roll up tightly and cut across the roll into very thin strips with a sharp knife.

Whisk the olive oil, vinegar, salt and pepper in a large bowl. Add the endive and toss well. Add the bacon and omelette, toss well and serve. **Serves four**

waxy hot potatoes contrast with **fruity black** olives and **flakes** of fish

**main players:**

*1 1/4 pounds waxy potatoes*

*3 cups canned tuna in olive oil*

*20 small black olives*

**supporting cast:**

*4 tablespoons extra-virgin olive oil*

*4 tablespoons white wine*

*2 tablespoons white wine vinegar*

*sea salt and freshly ground black pepper*

Cook the potatoes, unpeeled, in simmering, salted water until tender. Whisk the olive oil, white wine, vinegar, salt and pepper together in a large bowl until slightly thickened. Drain the tuna, and flake it with a fork into bite-size pieces.

Drain the potatoes and peel off the skin as soon as you can handle them – or don't bother peeling them at all – and cut into thick slices.

Toss the still-warm potatoes in the dressing. Using a pair of tongs, stack a few slices of potato on each plate. Top with a large spoonful of tuna so that it tumbles down the sides. Tuck in a few olives, and drizzle with any remaining dressing. **Serves four**

potato

olive

tuna

# Japanese peppered tuna, served rare on cold noodles with the surprise of creamy avocado

**main players:**

*2 x 9-ounce trimmed lengths*

*  sashimi-grade tuna*

*7 ounces dried soba noodles*

*1 avocado*

**supporting cast:**

*1 teaspoon sea salt*

*1/2 teaspoon freshly ground black pepper*

*1 teaspoon Japanese sansho pepper*

*2 tablespoons vegetable oil*

*2 tablespoons mirin*

*2 tablespoons soy sauce*

*1 tablespoon rice wine vinegar or*

*  white wine vinegar*

*1 teaspoon sesame oil, plus extra to serve*

Roll the tuna in the salt, pepper and sansho pepper. Heat the vegetable oil in a nonstick frying pan until quite hot and sear the tuna for 30 seconds on each side. Remove from the heat and let rest for 30 minutes.

Cook the soba noodles in a large pot of simmering water for 6–8 minutes or according to the instructions on the package, until cooked but still firm, as for spaghetti. Drain well, rinse under cold running water and set aside.

Mix the mirin, soy sauce, vinegar and sesame oil in a large bowl, add the drained noodles and toss well.

Cut the avocado in half lengthwise and twist the two halves apart. Hit the pit with the blade of a large knife, then turn the knife to twist out the pit. Peel off the skin, cut the flesh into small cubes and toss lightly through the noodles.

Arrange the noodles in mounds on four small dinner plates. Thinly slice the tuna, and arrange 3 or 4 slices on top. Drizzle with a little extra sesame oil and serve.

**Serves four**

Sashimi-grade tuna is super-fresh and trimmed in neat blocks ready for cutting. It is available from specialty food shops, top-quality fish shops and Japanese food stores.

tuna

noodles

avocado

# the slight bitterness of radicchio marries well with the saltiness of pancetta and the sweet-sourness of balsamic vinegar

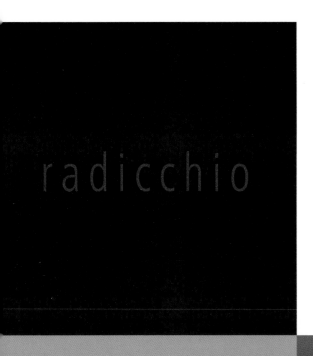

radicchio

bread

pancetta

**main players:**

*3 heads radicchio*

*6 thick slices good country bread*

*6 slices pancetta or prosciutto*

**supporting cast:**

*4 tablespoons extra-virgin olive oil, plus extra*

  *for bread*

*2 tablespoons balsamic or red wine vinegar*

*sea salt and freshly ground black pepper*

Mix the olive oil, salt and pepper together to make a dressing.

Cut each radicchio in half lengthwise through the stem, then push down on the stems with the heel of your hand so they are slightly flattened out. Brush with the dressing. Broil for 1–2 minutes, until they wilt, turning so that the outer leaves do not burn, but the inside still gets warm.

Brush the bread with a little extra olive oil and broil quickly on both sides. Arrange the toasted bread on serving plates. Broil the pancetta for 15 seconds, until just warm. Layer the pancetta and radicchio on top of the grilled bread and drizzle the vinegar on top. **Serves six**

trout

egg

potato

# hard-boiled eggs play off the richness of smoked trout and potatoes

**main players:**

*1 pound smoked trout fillets*

*1 pound potatoes*

*4 eggs*

**supporting cast:**

*sea salt*

*4 tablespoons extra-virgin olive oil*

*2 tablespoons lemon juice*

*1 teaspoon Dijon mustard*

*1 tablespoon tiny salted capers, rinsed*

Use your fingers to flake the smoked trout into bite-size pieces, carefully removing any skin and small bones.

Place the potatoes in a pot of cold water, add salt and bring to a boil. Simmer for 20 minutes or until tender. Remove from the heat and drain.

Meanwhile, place the eggs in a pot of simmering water and cook for 8–9 minutes until hard-boiled. Remove and cool under cold running water. Peel and slice lengthwise, then set aside. Cut the potatoes into thick slices – peel them first if you like, but don't feel you have to.

Whisk the olive oil, lemon juice, mustard and capers in a bowl, and gently toss the potatoes in the dressing to coat.

Arrange stacked layers of potato and hard-boiled egg slices in the center of each plate, top with the smoked trout and spoon any remaining dressing over.

**Serves four**

drained yogurt turns into a **fresh herb cheese** overnight to be served with roasted, **jewel-colored** peppers

**main players:**

*5 cups plain yogurt*

*3 mixed red and yellow peppers*

*8 sprigs fresh thyme*

**supporting cast:**

*2 tablespoons extra-virgin olive oil*

*1 teaspoon dried mint*

*20 small black olives*

*sea salt and freshly ground black pepper*

*toasted sourdough or warm Turkish bread*

  *to serve*

Arrange a doubled piece of dampened cheesecloth over a bowl and tip the yogurt into it. Gather up the edges, tie with string and hang over the bowl for 6 hours or overnight, allowing the liquid to drip out.

Heat the oven to 400°F. Place the peppers on a baking sheet and drizzle olive oil on top. Bake for 30 minutes until scorched and blistered. Place the peppers in a covered bowl for 10 minutes until cool enough to handle, then peel off the skins. Cut in half and discard the core and seeds. Cut the peppers lengthwise into wide strips.

Strip the thyme leaves from the stems. Untie the yogurt and mix with the thyme leaves, dried mint, salt and pepper.

Arrange the mixed peppers on each plate and top with a big spoonful of yogurt cheese. Scatter with small black olives. Serve with toasted sourdough bread or warmed Turkish bread. **Serves four**

yogurt

pepper

thyme

# snappy green beans and earthy artichoke hearts in a nutty dressing with extra crunch

beans

artichoke

walnut

**main players:**

*8 ounces fresh green beans, trimmed*

*6 artichoke hearts, preserved in oil*

*6 ounces walnut pieces*

**supporting cast:**

*3 tablespoons walnut oil or olive oil*

*1 tablespoon red wine vinegar*

*sea salt and freshly ground black pepper*

Cook the green beans in simmering, salted water, uncovered, for about 4 minutes, until tender. Drain and cool under cold running water.

Heat the broiler and broil the artichoke hearts, flat side to the heat, until lightly scorched and warmed through.

Toast the walnuts in a dry frying pan until warm and fragrant.

Whisk the oil and vinegar with salt and pepper, and throw in the beans, tossing well to coat thoroughly.

To assemble, arrange half the green beans in the center of a large serving plate, and top with a layer of artichoke hearts, grilled side up. Add a layer of remaining beans and scatter with the walnuts.

**Serves four**

# red onion

## beet

## corn

# warm roasted vegetables in a drizzle of capers and mustard – and you even get to eat the beet leaves

**main players:**

*2 red onions*

*2 bunches medium beets with stems*

*2 ears corn*

**supporting cast:**

*4 tablespoons extra-virgin olive oil*

*1 tablespoon red wine vinegar or*

*balsamic vinegar*

*1 tablespoon tiny capers, rinsed*

*1 teaspoon Dijon mustard*

*sea salt and freshly ground black pepper*

Heat the oven to 400°F. Peel the onions and cut in half, then cut each half into three wedges. Cut the stems from the beets and wash the stems thoroughly to remove any grit. Scrub the beets but don't peel. Remove the husks from the corn and cut in half, crosswise.

Arrange the beets, corn and onion wedges in a roasting pan. Drizzle with a little of the olive oil, sprinkle with salt and pepper and bake for 1 hour, turning occasionally until tender and slightly caramelized.

Remove from the oven and allow to cool for 10 minutes or so. Rub the skins off the beets and trim if necessary. Whisk the remaining olive oil with the vinegar, capers and mustard and add salt and pepper to taste.

Cook the beet greens in a pot of simmering, salted water for 5 minutes until wilted. Drain well – really well – and divide between plates.

Arrange the corn, beets and onions on each plate. Spoon the dressing on top and serve still warm or at room temperature.
**Serves four**

# Take the kitchen clock off the wall

and see what happens. Instead of sticking to the rigid hierarchies of lunch and dinner, you will immediately want to snack. This is a good thing. Snacks move easily from day to night; am to pm; breakfast to supper and back again. This is food you can dress up or down to suit. It's a return to primitive times, when humans were nomadic hunter-gatherers. Now, we forage in the refrigerator and the cupboard instead of the forests and fields. So let yourself go. Eat what you like, when you like. One of life's greatest pleasures is leftover chocolate mousse cake for breakfast, another is a fresh, juicy oyster at midnight. If you have no idea what the time is, just serve smoked salmon on toast. Besides, who says that eating three rich courses in a glamorous restaurant just before going to bed is good for you? Or that we thrive on greasy fried food within half an hour of waking up? Put that way, eating normal meals at normal mealtimes sounds completely abnormal.

# snacks

chicken

ginger

paper

# yes, paper, to wrap up fragrantly scented,
## tender chicken wings

**main players:**

*6 medium chicken wings*

*2-inch piece of ginger, peeled*

*6 squares thick greaseproof or parchment paper,*
*    measuring 12 x 8 inches*

**supporting cast:**

*3 tablespoons soy sauce*

*3 tablespoons Chinese rice wine or dry sherry*

*1 teaspoon sesame oil, plus extra for parcels*

*1/2 teaspoon salt*

*1/2 teaspoon sugar*

*peanut or vegetable oil for deep-frying*

Cut the tips off the chicken wings, then cut each wing at the joint and trim into two neat pieces. Cut the ginger into cubes and push through a garlic press, to give 1 tablespoon of ginger juice.

Mix the ginger juice, soy, rice wine, sesame oil, salt and sugar, and marinate the chicken pieces in the mixture for 3–4 hours, stirring every now and then.

Lay out one square of paper (use two if the paper is very thin) at an angle so that a corner is facing you, and brush the center lightly with sesame oil.

Place a well-drained chicken piece, skin-side down, in the center and bring the left corner in to fold over the chicken, creating a straight left side. Fold in the top corner, creating a straight side, then the bottom corner. Roll over and tuck in the remaining right hand corner to seal the parcel.

Heat the peanut oil until very hot and fry a few parcels at a time, for about 7 minutes, turning them as they cook.

Pile the chicken, still in its wrappers, on a large platter, and serve as a snack, with finger bowls. **Makes twelve**

a simple Spanish tapas snack of melting potatoes and spicy sausage, in paprika-hot juices

chorizo

potato

onion

**main players:**

*1 fresh chorizo sausage*

*1 pound potatoes*

*1 onion*

**supporting cast:**

*2 tablespoons extra-virgin olive oil*

*1 garlic clove, peeled and crushed*

*sea salt and freshly ground black pepper*

Cut the chorizo sausage into thick slices. Peel and finely chop the potatoes and onion.

Heat the olive oil in a frying pan and cook the chorizo, onion and garlic over moderate heat for 10 minutes, stirring, until the onion is lightly golden.

Add the potatoes and mix well. Add the salt, pepper and enough water to cover, then cook over medium heat for 30 minutes until the water reduces to a thickened sauce and the potatoes are tender. Serve with crusty bread.

**Serves four**

# wok-fried, peppery squid, to serve with an icy-cold beer

**main players:**

*1 pound cleaned squid tubes*

*1 teaspoon ground Sichuan or black*

*  peppercorns*

*5 whole dried chiles*

**supporting cast:**

*1 teaspoon sea salt, plus extra to serve*

*3/4 cup cornstarch or all-purpose flour*

*vegetable oil for deep-frying*

Clean the squid tubes well and peel off any skin. Cut in half lengthwise, then cut into pieces measuring 1 x 2 inches and use the tip of a sharp knife to score an even row of lines in the outer skin. This will make the squid curl up when fried.

Heat the wok and toast the peppercorns and 1 of the dried chiles until hot and fragrant. Place the peppercorns, chile and salt in a mortar or a tough little bowl. Crush to a powder with a pestle or a wooden spoon and combine with the cornstarch.

Heat the vegetable oil until smoking. Toss the squid in the seasoned flour and shake off the excess. Fry the squid for about 1 minute (beware of spitting oil), then drain well on paper towels.

When the squid is cooked, deep-fry the remaining whole dried chiles until they turn crisp and dark (these are more for effect than for eating). Pile the squid high on a plate and top with the fried chiles. Sprinkle with a little extra sea salt.

**Serves four**

If you can find banana leaves, wipe them clean, cut into squares and roll into cones for serving, fastened with bamboo skewers.

squid

pepper

chile

soft, fresh balls of cheese hit with **enough heat** to melt gently over **fragrant lemon** leaves, sparked up with a basil-green pesto

**main players:**

1 large bunch basil

8 large lemon leaves

2 balls mozzarella cheese, preferably

buffalo milk

**supporting cast:**

2 tablespoons pine nuts

2 tablespoons grated Parmesan cheese

1/2 cup extra-virgin olive oil, plus extra

for leaves

sea salt

Remove the basil leaves from their stems, and place in the food processor with the pine nuts and Parmesan. With the motor running, slowly add enough olive oil to make a fresh green paste. Add a little salt. The pesto can be stored in an airtight jar until needed.

Heat the broiler or a cast-iron griddle. Wash and dry the lemon leaves, then brush both sides with a little olive oil. Thinly slice the mozzarella and place one or two slices on each lemon leaf. Brush lightly with olive oil.

Broil or griddle until the heat causes the cheese to softly melt. Remove from the heat, top each leaf with a teaspoon of pesto and serve. You don't eat the leaf, okay? It's just there to give a smoky, lemony tang to the cheese.

**Serves four**

basil

lemon leaf

cheese

# lettuce

# scallops

# shrimp

crisp and crunchy shrimp and mushrooms served in a lettuce cup to eat **in your hands**

**main players:**

1 head iceberg lettuce

12 large raw scallops

12 medium raw shrimp

**supporting cast:**

10 dried shiitake mushrooms

2 tablespoons peanut oil

4 tablespoons chopped water chestnuts

3 tablespoons oyster sauce

Soak the mushrooms in 1 cup of hot water for 30 minutes. Carefully separate 4 cup-shaped leaves from the lettuce, wash, dry and chill until required.

Wash and dry the scallops. Devein the shrimp by hooking out the black intestinal tract through the back of each with a fine bamboo skewer. Peel, then chop into rough cubes. Drain the mushrooms, reserving the

water, trim off the stems and thinly slice the caps.

Heat the peanut oil in a wok until it starts to smoke. Add the shrimp and scallops and cook for 15 seconds, tossing like mad. Add the water chestnuts and mushrooms and toss through.

Add the oyster sauce, stirring, and a little of the mushroom water if you need more sauce. Spoon the mixture into the chilled lettuce cups and serve immediately.

To eat, fold up the lettuce leaf and take a bite. **Makes four**

a simple mix of **marinated olives** brings the Mediterranean to the shores of your **cocktail glass**

olive

rosemary

garlic

**main players:**

*1 pound mixed olives in olive oil*

*8 sprigs rosemary or thyme*

*2 garlic cloves, peeled and crushed*

**supporting cast:**

*3 tablespoons extra-virgin olive oil*

*6 bay leaves*

*1 teaspoon dried oregano*

When shopping for olives, make a nuisance of yourself. Get some big black ones, shrunken black ones, green Spanish queen ones, and any other type you can find.

Warm the olive oil in a frying pan with the rosemary sprigs, garlic, bay leaves and oregano and cook gently, stirring, for 5 minutes to infuse the oil.

Add the olives and toss well to coat in the spiced oil, then cook gently, stirring occasionally, for 5–10 minutes until soft and shiny. Use a slotted spoon to transfer olives, garlic, bay leaves and herbs to a rustic serving dish and serve hot, warm or at room temperature. **Serves four to six**

# crisp wafers made of the noble Parmigiano-Reggiano are used to sandwich succulent slices of prosciutto and ripe figs

parmesan

prosciutto

fig

**main players:**

*2 cups freshly grated Parmesan cheese*

*8 slices prosciutto*

*2 ripe figs*

Heat the oven to 350°F. Lay an egg ring on a nonstick baking sheet. Sprinkle an even layer of grated Parmesan inside the ring. Remove the ring and use it to make a second wafer next to the first. No egg ring?

Just make two tidy circles about 4 inches across. Use these first two wafers as your guinea pigs, because you may have to adjust the heat of your oven to suit the rest.

Bake for 3–5 minutes, watching carefully, until the cheese has melted into a soft wafer shape. Remove from the oven while still bubbling and leave for 1 minute. Carefully lift off the wafers and lay them on a wire rack to cool and harden. Adjust the oven temperature if necessary and continue the process until you have 8 wafers.

To serve, cut the figs into quarters. Lay 2 slices of prosciutto on top of a Parmesan wafer on each of 4 plates. Top with 2 fig quarters and a final wafer, and serve.

**Serves four**

oysters

chile

black beans

lightly **steamed** oysters in their shell with the smoky, **earthy taste** of black bean and a little red chile

**main players:**

*12 freshly opened oysters*

*1 tablespoon Chinese black beans, rinsed*

*1 small red chile, finely chopped*

**supporting cast:**

*2 tablespoons Chinese rice wine or dry sherry*

*1/2 teaspoon sesame oil*

*2 tablespoons peanut oil*

Arrange the oysters, still in their shells, on a heatproof plate that fits in your steamer. (Crumple foil beneath them and nestle them in it so they don't tip over.)

Mash the well-rinsed and drained black beans lightly with the chile, rice wine and sesame oil. Divide the mixture equally between the oysters.

Bring the water in the steamer to a rolling boil and place the plate of oysters in the steamer. Cover and steam for 3–4 minutes, until the oysters plump up and start to give off their juices, but do not overcook.

Heat the peanut oil in a small pan until just smoking. Drizzle a little hot oil over each oyster. **Serves four**

Chinese salted black beans are available in Asian food stores.

fresh little rolls with a **hint of chile** will **save you** from being bored

**main players:**

*8 medium shrimp, raw or cooked*

*1 ripe avocado*

*8 rice paper wrappers*

**supporting cast:**

*2 tablespoons sweet chile sauce*

*sea salt and freshly ground black pepper*

shrimp

avocado          rice paper

Devein the raw shrimp by passing a thin bamboo skewer through the back and hooking out any thin black intestinal tract. If using raw shrimp, poach them gently in a pot of simmering, salted water for 3–4 minutes until just cooked. Drain, cool and peel. If using cooked shrimp, peel off the shells.

Cut the avocado in half lengthwise, remove the pit and peel. Cut the flesh into long strips.

Bring a pot of water to a boil and use tongs to dip the rice paper wrappers in and out of the water, one at a time. Lay them on a clean work surface, and top each with a shrimp, a couple of strips of avocado, a little sweet chile sauce to taste and a sprinkling of salt and pepper. Wrap up as if for a spring roll, tucking the ends in neatly as you go. Serve soon after making.

**Serves four**

It's late, and you haven't eaten for what seems like days. Don't stay out, go home. You can throw together a fast feast long before you can get a table at your favorite late-night haunt. If you can get a table.

Rice is good. Cheese is great. Toast is brilliant. Baconliness is close to godliness. The trick at supper is to eat exactly what you feel like eating. If that means three videos and take-out Chinese in bed, so be it. If it means a big bowl of pasta at the kitchen table, that's fine, too. If it means a glamorous post-opera supper and a seductive spread of dishes, well, go for it. Supper should either give you satisfaction at the end of the day, or the strength to prolong the evening into the night, should you want to do so. It's also very handy when you don't quite know what you want, but you know you want something. And you want it now.

# supper

cod

parsley

tomato

# fresh, fast, and cooked in just one pan

**main players:**

*4 x 5-ounce firm white-fleshed fish fillets,*

*such as cod or hake*

*1 small bunch flat-leaf parsley*

*1 pint cherry tomatoes*

**supporting cast:**

*2 tablespoons extra-virgin olive oil, plus*

*extra for serving*

*2 anchovy fillets*

*2 tablespoons small black olives*

*1 tablespoons tiny salted capers, rinsed*

Cut the fish fillets into nice chunky bite-size pieces and set aside. Set aside a few leaves of parsley for garnish and finely chop the rest until you have 2 tablespoons.

Heat the olive oil in a heavy-bottomed frying pan, add the anchovies and break them up with a wooden spoon. Add the fish and cook over medium heat, moving the chunks around the pan as they cook.

Add the tomatoes, olives and capers and gently cook until the tomatoes soften and start to burst out of their skins.

Add the finely chopped parsley, then serve in shallow pasta bowls. Scatter with the reserved parsley leaves and drizzle with a little extra olive oil. **Serves four**

# bitter endive hits it off with rich and elegant

## Gruyère and cream in a cheesy melting dish

**main players:**

*8 heads of Belgian endive*

*2 tablespoons grated Gruyère cheese*

*3 tablespoons heavy cream*

**supporting cast:**

*1 teaspoon butter*

*sea salt and freshly ground black pepper*

endive

gruyère

cream

Heat the oven to 350°F. Trim the endive ends neatly and cut in half lengthwise. Cook for 10 minutes in simmering, salted water until tender, then remove and drain.

Lightly butter an ovenproof gratin dish, and lay the endive in one layer, cut side down. Sprinkle with the cheese, salt and pepper, and spoon the cream on top.

Bake for 15–20 minutes until the cream is bubbling and lightly golden. **Serves four**

This works just as well with thin asparagus spears in season, topped with cream and grated Parmesan.

I call this **happy rice** – it's sunny, smily, mindlessly easy to make, and it takes me back to happy **holidays** in Spain

**main players:**

2 red peppers

5 ounces cooked ham

1 cup Arborio rice

**supporting cast**

2 red onions

1 pinch saffron threads

1/2 teaspoon paprika

2 tablespoons extra-virgin olive oil

2 cups hot chicken stock or water

sea salt and freshly ground black pepper

Heat the oven to 400°F. Roast the peppers for 30 minutes until scorched and blistered. Remove from the oven, cool slightly in a covered bowl and peel off the skins. Cut them in half, discard the core and seeds and cut the flesh into short strips.

Cut the ham into short strips. Peel and finely chop the red onions. Pound the saffron and paprika with a spoonful of hot water until dissolved.

Heat the oil in a frying pan and cook the onion over moderate heat for 10 minutes, stirring, until soft. Add the rice and toss to coat. Add the hot stock or water and the spice liquid, and bring to a boil.

Add the red peppers, ham and salt and pepper and stir well. Reduce the heat to low, cover and simmer for 20 minutes, stirring occasionally, until the rice is cooked and the liquid has been absorbed. Serve in bowls with a fork and spoon. **Serves four**

red pepper

ham

rice

# a quick Italian frittata of crispy bacon and lots of Parmesan tossed through pasta and pan-fried until golden

macaroni

bacon

parmesan

**main players:**

*12 ounces macaroni, penne or rigatoni*

*4 thin slices bacon*

*3 tablespoons grated Parmesan cheese, plus*

   *extra to serve*

**supporting cast:**

*6 eggs*

*sea salt and freshly ground black pepper*

Cook the pasta in plenty of boiling, salted water, according to the package instructions, until tender but still firm to the bite. Drain well, then rinse in cold water and drain well again.

Cut the bacon into short strips and fry in a nonstick frying pan until crisp. Remove the bacon with a slotted spoon, leaving the bacon fat in the pan.

Break the eggs into a large bowl and beat lightly. Add the cheese and stir. Add the drained pasta to the bowl and toss well. Add the bacon, salt and pepper and toss again.

Pour the egg and pasta mixture into the pan in which you cooked the bacon and cover. Cook over gentle heat for 15 minutes.

Check that the bottom is lightly golden and the top is set. If the top is still runny, put the pan under the broiler for 1 minute. Sprinkle the frittata with the extra Parmesan and serve hot, in big wedges.
**Serves four**

a **great trick** – throw in handfuls of fresh green leaves at the last minute to wilt into juicy greens that cut the strength of the **blue cheese**

linguine

arugula   gorgonzola

**main players:**

*5 ounces gorgonzola or other good blue cheese*

*2 bunches arugula*

*1 pound dried linguine or spaghettini*

**supporting cast:**

*1/2 cup milk*

*1 tablespoon butter*

*freshly ground black pepper*

Trim off the stems of the arugula, and wash and dry the leaves.

Mash or chop the cheese and set 1 tablespoon of it aside. Combine the remaining cheese in a pan with the milk, butter and pepper. Stir with a wooden spoon until the sauce melts together. Add a few spoonfuls of the pasta cooking water, stir through, and keep warm.

Cook the linguine in plenty of boiling, salted water, according to the package instructions, until tender but still firm to the bite. When the pasta is cooked, throw the arugula into the pasta pan for a few seconds until they wilt, then drain both the pasta and arugula together. Divide between four pasta bowls.

Spoon the hot sauce on top, toss lightly, and sprinkle with the reserved cheese.
**Serves four**

# green beans wok-tossed with a little spicy pork and a slow chile burn

**main players:**

*1 pound green beans or long snake beans*

*7 ounces minced pork*

*2 garlic cloves, peeled and crushed*

**supporting cast:**

*1 tablespoon soy sauce*

*1/2 teaspoon cornstarch*

*1 teaspoon sugar*

*3 tablespoons vegetable oil*

*1 tablespoon Chinese rice wine*

*1/2 teaspoon chile oil or less, to taste*

*sea salt and freshly ground black pepper*

Trim the tips off the beans and cut into 6-inch lengths. Cook in simmering, salted water for 2 minutes, then drain and cool under cold running water.

Mix the pork with the soy sauce, cornstarch, sugar, salt and pepper.

The trick to this dish is to have both the wok and the oil hot at all times, and to cook quickly, tossing constantly. Heat one-third of the vegetable oil in a wok. When hot, stir-fry the beans quickly with a pinch of salt for 1 minute over high heat, until wrinkled.

Remove the beans and reheat the wok, adding the remaining vegetable oil and the garlic cloves. When hot, discard the garlic and add the pork mixture, stir-frying quickly for 3 minutes until it darkens.

Add the rice wine and chile oil and stir through. Return the beans to the sauce and stir-fry briefly until mixed. Serve with plenty of steamed rice. **Serves four**

beans

pork

garlic

shrimp

tofu

# steamed blocks of tofu topped with fresh shrimp – a light, healthy meal put together in minutes

onion

**main players:**

*12 small raw shrimp*

*8 small blocks fresh tofu*

*2 green onions, finely chopped*

**supporting cast:**

*4 tablespoons soy sauce*

*1 tablespoon sesame oil*

*1 tablespoon oyster sauce*

*1 tablespoon sweet chile sauce*

*1 tablespoon crisp-fried shallots (optional)*

Devein the shrimp by inserting a fine bamboo skewer through the back and hooking out any black intestinal tract. Peel them, leaving the tails on.

Drain the tofu and stack one block on top of another until you have four two-story blocks. Arrange them on a flat heatproof plate that will fit into your steamer. Place the shrimp on top or in a separate steamer.

Steam over bubbling water for 5 minutes, until the tofu is heated through and the shrimp are just cooked, turning from transparent to opaque.

In the meantime, combine the soy sauce, sesame oil, oyster sauce and chile sauce in a small pan and heat, stirring, without boiling.

To serve, use a spatula to carefully place a block of tofu on each plate. Arrange the shrimp on top. Spoon the hot sauce over and scatter with green onions and fried shallots, if using. **Serves four**

# beans

## prosciutto

## polenta

**tender** fava beans spooned generously over foothills of **golden** polenta.

**main players:**

2 pounds fava beans, shelled

4 slices prosciutto

12 ounces instant polenta

**supporting cast:**

2 tablespoons extra-virgin olive oil

2 onions, finely chopped

1 cup chicken stock

1 tablespoon butter

sea salt and freshly ground black pepper

freshly grated Parmesan cheese to serve

Heat the oil in a heavy-bottomed frying pan, add the onions and cook until they soften. Add the fava beans, salt, pepper and chicken stock. Cover and cook gently for 15 minutes, until the beans are tender and there are barely any juices. Cut the prosciutto into strips, add to the beans and cook for 1 minute.

To make the polenta, bring 6 cups water seasoned with 1/2 teaspoon salt to a boil. Stirring constantly, pour in the instant polenta in a slow, steady stream, like sand. Reduce the heat to very low, and stir with a wooden spoon for 6–8 minutes, until the polenta pulls away from the sides of the pan. Stir in the butter, then taste. Add pepper, and more salt to taste.

Spoon huge dollops of polenta on each warmed serving plate, and then top with the fava bean and prosciutto mixture. Sprinkle with grated Parmesan and serve.
**Serves four**

# a simple fried egg turns spaghetti into supper

**main players:**

*14 ounces spaghetti or tagliatelle*

*4 eggs*

*1 handful sage leaves*

**supporting cast:**

*2 tablespoons olive oil, plus extra for pasta*

*1 tablespoon butter*

*Parmesan cheese for shaving and grating*

*sea salt and freshly ground pepper*

Cook the pasta in plenty of boiling, salted water, according to the package instructions, until firm but tender to the bite. Towards the end of the cooking time, heat half of the olive oil and the butter in a nonstick frying pan. Crack the eggs carefully into the pan, cover and cook gently until the whites have set and the yolks are cooked but still runny.

Using a vegetable peeler, shave off 8–12 curls of cheese and set aside. Grate 2 tablespoons of cheese and set aside.

Drain the pasta well and divide between four pasta bowls. Toss with a little extra olive oil, the grated cheese and salt and pepper, and top each one with a fried egg (you may have to cut any joined ones apart). Top with the Parmesan curls.

Heat the remaining olive oil and very quickly sizzle the sage leaves until crisp. Pour the oil and sage leaves over the pasta and serve immediately. Serve the remaining wedge of Parmesan at the table with a small hand grater. **Serves four**

spaghetti

egg

sage

# a great big poached sausage, sliced over juicy, spicy, herby lentils

**main players:**

*1¹/₂ cups brown or green lentils, soaked for*

*30 minutes*

*1 large smoked sausage, such as Saucisse*

*Lyonnaise, or 4 smaller ones*

*1 bunch flat-leaf parsley, finely chopped*

**supporting cast:**

*2 tablespoons extra-virgin olive oil*

*1 onion, finely chopped*

*14-ounce can plum (roma) tomatoes*

*¹/₂ teaspoon ground coriander*

*¹/₂ teaspoon ground cumin*

*sea salt and freshly ground black pepper*

Heat the olive oil in a pan, add the onion and cook for 15 minutes over a moderate heat until soft. Add the tomatoes and their juices, drained lentils, coriander, cumin, salt, pepper and 2 cups cold water, and bring to a boil, stirring. Reduce the heat to low and cook for 30 minutes until lentils are tender.

Prick the sausage and poach in simmering water for 20 minutes to heat through.

Stir most of the chopped parsley into the lentils and divide them between four plates. Drain the sausage, peel off and discard the skin and slice into thick rounds. Arrange the slices on the lentils and serve with the remaining parsley on top. **Serves four**

sausage

parsley

lentils

There are things that lie patiently around the house – like onions and garlic – until you need them. Or things you buy every few days – like bread and lemons – that can actually feed you in many ways. Or things that you can't live without – like tomatoes and olive oil – that can bring your cooking to life. Treat this chapter as if it's that lovely, kind, but missing person in your life who is always on call to answer all those boring questions you're too embarassed to ask anyone else, like how to peel a tomato, make a Caesar salad dressing or poach the perfect egg.

wine

bread

eggs

olive oil

onions

lemons

tomatoes

# standards

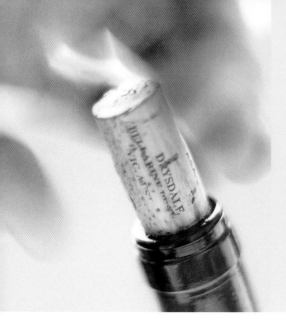

# bread, cheese and wine... bliss

## wine

It's time we took to the bottle and treated wine as a great ingredient, using its layers of flavors to brighten our cooking in any number of ways, not the least by the glass, direct to the cook. Begin with a good splash of white or red wine, and allow it to bubble and reduce to one quarter its volume. This way, the alcohol evaporates, and you are left with lots of flavor to add to casseroles, soups and sauces.

**As a flavor zapper:** Use red and white wine for stews, poaching and marinades, but don't stop there. Use *shao hsing* (Chinese rice wine) for marinating chicken and for Chinese cooking and sake (Japanese rice wine) for Japanese marinades and sauces.

**As a salad dressing:** Start with a good vinegar (wine, Champagne, sherry) in a bowl. Add a pinch of sea salt and a grind of black pepper. Whisk in a splash of dry white wine or Champagne and a few chopped herbs, then drizzle in extra-virgin olive oil or a good nut oil, whisking constantly.

**As a poaching liquid:** Poach fish, prawns and crab in a broth of one part white wine to four parts water, along with diced carrot, celery and parsley.

**As a sauce:** Deglaze a cooking pan by splashing some wine into the hot pan and scraping up the crusty sediments left after browning chicken or lamb. Bring it to a boil, stirring, then strain. Whisk in a little butter for richness and serve.

**As a meal:** Bread, cheese and wine. Bliss. Try crusty sourdough with Manchego cheese and a red Rioja; dark rye with goat cheese and Gewürztraminer; or toasted sweet brioche with gorgonzola and Sauternes.

**Spiced pears**

Combine $1\frac{1}{4}$ cups sugar, $2\frac{1}{2}$ cups red wine, 2 cups water, 2 cinnamon sticks, and a few cloves and peppercorns, and bring to a boil, stirring. Boil for 1 minute, then remove from the heat. Peel 6 pears lengthwise, leaving the stem, cut out the base core, and place snugly in the liquid. Simmer gently for 30 minutes or until the pears are tender, then leave to cool in the syrup. Serve with fresh cream, ricotta cheese or coffee ice cream, or slice and serve with duck and lamb.

**Summer/winter marinade**

Combine $\frac{1}{2}$ cup white wine, 3 tablespoons olive oil, 1 crushed garlic clove, 1 tablespoon chopped parsley, sea salt and pepper to marinate fish, chicken, lamb or beef for summer grilling. Change to red wine in winter to give flavor to lean meats such as chicken and rabbit before some long, slow cooking.

# bread

Great bread has a life longer than the day you buy it. It can live again and again, drowned in soups; dunked in hot, milky coffee; baked with eggs and milk; torn into pieces and tossed with olive oil, tomatoes and olives. So start with good bread: tough sourdough, rich brioche, strong Italian casalinga bread, ciabatta, pita, focaccia and fragile French ficelle.

**As a snack:** Toast thick door-stopper slices of slightly stale Italian casalinga bread and top with herb-strewn mushrooms, chicken livers or baked beans.

**As a sauce:** Heat milk, butter, cloves, herbs and a chopped onion to boiling point, then leave until cool. Strain and whisk in fresh white bread crumbs until thick but still liquid. Serve with roasted chicken.

**As a salad:** Cut thick fingers of country-style bread and fry with finely chopped bacon until crisp. Toss into a salad of torn green leaves with a dressing of mustard, red wine vinegar, garlic and olive oil.

**As a soup:** Cover thick slices of sourdough bread with thin slices of Gruyère cheese and grill until melting. Place in soup bowls and pour a good chicken soup on top. Sprinkle with parsley.

**As a crumb:** Turn stale bread into chunky crumbs that beat hands down the sawdust sold by that name in supermarkets. Cut off the crusts and cut the bread into chunks. Leave on a baking sheet in a very low oven until completely dry, without browning. Cool and process briefly in a food processor, or crush by hand and store in an airtight jar until you're ready for them.

**French toast**

Dip 4 long slices of baguette, cut on the diagonal, into a batter of 2 eggs, $1/2$ cup milk and a little ground cinnamon. Fry quickly in a little butter on both sides until crisp and golden. Serve with a drizzle of honey, a dusting of confectioner's sugar, fresh sliced fruits or a handful of berries.

**Italian bread salad**

Toast 2 thick slices of country-style bread and cut into cubes. Peel 3 ripe tomatoes and roughly chop. Combine with 1 finely chopped red pepper, 1 tablespoon rinsed capers, 1 crushed garlic clove, 2 anchovy fillets, 1 tablespoon black olives, 2 tablespoons red wine vinegar and 3 tablespoons extra-virgin olive oil. Toss the bread in the salad and serve at room temperature.

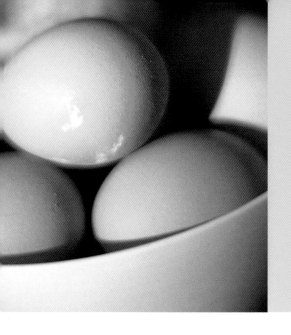

top anything with a perfectly poached egg

# eggs

Eggs are the pale and beautiful symbols of purity, rebirth and instant gratification. One crack, and you have breakfast. Another crack, and a sauce is bound, a soufflé rises, a cake is baked and fresh pasta lies hanging from the broom handle. Use free-range eggs, because I don't care what they say, I know the hens are happier.

**As a stew:** Break a few eggs on top of a baked Mediterranean vegetable stew (eggplant, zucchini, tomatoes) and return to the oven until almost set.

**As a soup:** Heat a good chicken stock to a high simmer. Beat 2 eggs and slowly pour them into the broth, whisking constantly, letting them cook into long thin strands. Sprinkle with parsley and serve with garlicky toasted bread.

**As a sandwich:** Mash a few hard-boiled eggs with sea salt, pepper and very good mayonnaise while still warm, then spread on fresh white or rye bread.

**As a garnish:** Make a really thin omelet in a wok or frying pan with 3 eggs flavored with a little soy sauce. Roll it up, cut into thin strips, and use as a garnish for noodles, soups and stir-fries.

**As a snack:** Hard-boil two dozen quail eggs and serve peeled with a little spiced salt (try cumin or paprika) for dipping and chilled Champagne for sipping.

**As a hangover cure:** Combine 1 fresh, raw egg yolk, a splash of brandy, a shake of Tabasco, a squeeze of lemon juice and a grind of pepper and down it in one gulp. This is the only good reason to give up drinking that I have yet come across.

**The perfect poached egg**

Fill a broad, shallow pan with water and bring to a boil. Add 2 tablespoons white vinegar and turn off the heat. Break open 4 eggs and slip them quickly into the water one at a time. Cover and leave for 3 minutes. Remove the eggs from the water with a slotted spoon and drain on paper towels. Trim off any rough edges with scissors, and serve.

**The perfect omelet**

Lightly beat 3 eggs, sea salt and pepper together with a fork. Add 1 teaspoon butter to a good pan. When it foams, add the eggs and stir lightly with a fork over high heat. Use the fork to lift the edges as they set and tilt the pan to allow the runny egg to spill down into the gap. Add any fillings at the last minute, then slide onto a warm plate and jerk the pan so that one side folds over as you tip it. Serve immediately.

# olive oil

Olive oil is the new butter, but there is room for both in our kitchens and on our tables. If we spent as much on one bottle of extra-virgin olive oil from Italy, Spain or Greece as we spent on a decent bottle of wine, we'd have joy for a month or two instead of for an hour or two. Better still, we'd remember using it.

**As a mash:** The next time you mash spuds, use extra-virgin olive oil (at room temperature, don't heat it first) instead of butter. Gorgeous.

**As a relish:** Keep your best olive oil on the table and drizzle lightly over fresh vegetable and bean soups, pasta, and roasted vegetables.

**As a pasta sauce:** Chop 6 ripe tomatoes and combine in a pan with 1/2 cup extra-virgin olive oil, lots of fresh basil, a little garlic, sea salt and black pepper, and cook, stirring gently, for 15 minutes. Toss with your favorite pasta.

**As a marinade:** Combine garlic, chopped parsley and coriander, lemon juice, ground cumin, paprika, sea salt and pepper with extra-virgin olive oil and use to marinate fish, prawns, lobster, lamb chops or chicken wings before grilling.

**As a salad dressing:** Whisk extra-virgin olive oil with white wine or sherry vinegar, sea salt and pepper and a little Dijon mustard.

**As a vegetable dressing:** Whisk extra-virgin olive oil and red wine vinegar with sea salt, pepper, rinsed capers, fresh thyme, oregano and pine nuts.

**Spaghetti with olive oil, garlic and chile**

Cook 14 ounces spaghetti in boiling, salted water until firm but tender to the bite. Heat 4 tablespoons extra-virgin olive oil in a heavy pan, add 4 crushed garlic cloves and 1 chopped red chile, and warm through. Drain spaghetti, pour oil mixture on top, add some chopped parsley and serve.

**Fresh herb mayonnaise**

Process 2 egg yolks and 1 tablespoon lemon juice in a food processor, and add up to 1 1/2 cups olive oil very slowly, drop by drop, with the motor running, until half the oil has been incorporated. Now you can add it a little faster in a slow, steady stream, still processing, until you have a thick, creamy paste. Add sea salt, pepper, and more lemon juice to taste. Finely chop fresh basil, thyme or chives and fold through the mayonnaise. Serve with eggs, cold meats, vegetables and fish.

# onions can save your life

## onions

If you get home hungry, just put a frying pan on the stove. Throw in a little olive oil, a couple of crushed garlic cloves and a finely chopped onion or two. Get all that sizzling, then work out what you can turn it into.

**As a stew:** Add chicken pieces, white wine, chicken stock and beans and cook until tender.

**As a pasta sauce:** Add a few roughly chopped and skinned pork sausages and a can of tomatoes, cook until thick and dump onto bowls of pasta.

**As a supper:** Add some chopped fresh tomatoes and herbs and cook until stewy, then serve as a sauce poured over grilled slices of eggplant, zucchini and red peppers.

**Sweet onion confit**

Slice 4 big white onions finely and cook in 2 tablespoons butter and 2 cups dry white wine in a heavy-bottomed pan over low heat for 30 minutes, covered, until the onion is soft and melting. Add sea salt and pepper to taste. To use as a relish, cook, uncovered, until the liquid has evaporated. To use as a creamy sauce, add 1/2 cup hot chicken stock or water and cook for another 5 minutes.

**As a risotto:** Add Arborio rice and toss to coat. Add some peas, then slowly add chicken stock and cook slowly for 30–40 minutes, stirring often. Serve with plenty of freshly grated Parmesan cheese.

**As a soup:** Add finely chopped leeks, carrots, potatoes and celery, cover with boiling water and cook until soupy.

**Onion and black olive frittata**

Slice 3 big white onions finely and cook in 1 tablespoon butter for 30 minutes over low heat until soft and melting, then cool. Arrange in a thick layer in a lightly oiled quiche pan and sprinkle with 2 tablespoons pitted black olives. Beat 4 eggs with 1 cup cream and 1 cup milk. Add salt, pepper and ground nutmeg and pour on top. Bake at 350° F for 45 minutes until puffy and golden. Serve warm.

**As a flavorful topping:** Add minced veal, chopped bacon, white wine, tomatoes, nutmeg, a little flour and cook for 1 hour, stirring, then serve on top of polenta, pasta, rice or toasted bread.

# get bitter and twisted **with a lemon**

## lemons

Lemons are why our mouths water. Use them to zap up grilled vegetables, make cocktails and spike up sauces and dressings. Get bitter and twisted and give your taste buds a big dipper ride. There's no point being sweet if you can't be sour as well.

**As a dressing:** Whisk 4 tablespoons lemon juice with 5 tablespoons extra-virgin olive oil, sea salt, freshly ground black pepper and 1 tablespoon finely chopped parsley and drizzle over shellfish, vegetables or mixed green leaves.

**As a marinade**: Combine $1/2$ cup white wine, 2 tablespoons lemon juice, 2 tablespoons olive oil, 1 crushed garlic clove, 1 tablespoon chopped parsley, sea salt and pepper and use to marinate fish, chicken, lamb or beef for summer grilling.

**As a margarita:** Shake 3 tablespoons lemon juice with 3 tablespoons tequila, 2 tablespoons Cointreau, and 3 tablespoons lime cordial with crushed ice, and serve immediately. Makes one.

**As an appetizer:** This is weird, but cute. Slice 2 lemons and chill the slices well. Arrange on a tray and top each slice with 1 teaspoon of salmon caviar. Top with a little sprig of dill and serve with shot glasses of frozen sake or vodka. You just suck the caviar off the lemon and discard the lemon.

**As an accompaniment:** When grilling or sautéing shellfish or fish, grill or sauté a few slices or halves of lemon as well, to serve at the same time.

**As a cleaning agent**: Rub half a cut lemon over your chopping board to eat up the odors of onion, garlic and fish.

**Lemon butter sauce**

Combine 2 tablespoons lemon juice with 3 tablespoons chicken or vegetable stock in a small saucepan and heat, stirring. When hot, whisk in $1/2$ cup cold butter, a few small pieces at a time, without allowing the sauce to boil. Taste for lemon juice, salt and pepper, and serve over asparagus, salmon or chicken.

**Caesar salad dressing**

Place 1 egg in simmering water for 1 minute, then remove, crack into a bowl, and whisk with 2 tablespoons lemon juice, sea salt, pepper, and $1/2$ cup extra-virgin olive oil until smooth. Add 1 tablespoon grated Parmesan and 2 finely chopped anchovies, and drizzle over crisp romaine leaves.

# bite into a fresh
# ripe red
## tomato

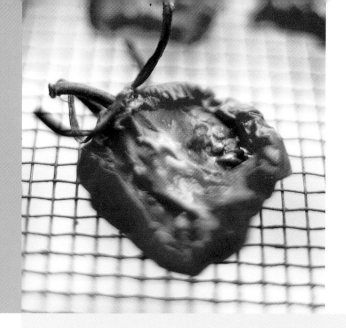

## tomatoes

Go berserk with them when they're in season and go to the canned ones when they're not. If you have a spare hour, roast a few in the oven to intensify their flavor, for sauces, pasta or to go with grilled meat or a roast. Or just bite into a fresh, ripe red tomato as if it were an apple.

**As a salad:** Slice a large red or yellow tomato into four slices, then reassemble, layering fresh basil leaves and fresh mozzarella cheese between each slice. Dress with extra-virgin olive oil, sea salt, pepper and balsamic vinegar.

**As a roast:** Cut a heap of plum (roma) tomatoes in half, drizzle with extra-virgin olive oil and roast in a low oven for 1 hour. Serve with fresh ricotta cheese and pesto.

**Oven-dried tomatoes**
Cut 2 pounds plum (roma) tomatoes in three lengthwise slices, salt very lightly and bake in a single layer in a very low oven (180°F) for 10 hours or overnight until semi – but not fully – dried. Store in an airtight jar, covered in olive oil (pressing down firmly to remove any air) and eat within a week, with crusty bread and cheese, in salads, pasta or on toast.

**As peeled:** Cut lightly around the circumference with the tip of a sharp knife and dunk in a pot of simmering water for 10 seconds. Remove and peel off the skin.

**As a fine dice:** Peel the tomatoes and cut in half. Squeeze out the seeds and juice, and cut the flesh into small dice.

**Tomato jam**
Cut 2 pounds tomatoes in half, squeeze out the seeds, then roughly chop the flesh. Place in a saucepan with 2 tablespoons brown sugar, 2 tablespoons mustard seeds, 2 tablespoons red wine vinegar and 3 table-spoons olive oil and bring to a boil. Lower the heat and simmer, bubbling, for up to 1 hour, stirring occasionally, until thick and jammy. Add salt and pepper, cool and store in airtight jars in the fridge. Use within a week.

**As a fry**: Cut big beefsteak tomatoes into thick slices and fry briskly in a nonstick pan with a touch of olive oil until scorched. Stack with fried eggs, fresh thyme and crisp bacon.

**As a sauce:** Toss a basket of cherry tomatoes into a frying pan with a little olive oil and garlic and cook until they burst and soften. Use for lamb, pasta and tuna.

# Index

# Index by group